世界横行柔道武者修業

A Judo Warrior's Journey Around the Globe
Volume 1: America 1904~1907

The Dispatches of Kodokan Yondan
前田光世 Maeda Mitsuyo
Edited by 薄田斬雲 Usuda Zanun

Translated by シャハン・エリック Eric Shahan
Foreword by ヴァーゴ・キース Keith Vargo

Copyright © 2022 Eric Michael Shahan
All Rights Reserved.
ISBN: 978-1-950959-56-3

A JUDO WARRIOR'S JOURNEY AROUND THE GLOBE・世界横行柔道武者修業

Translator's Introduction

The correspondences of Maeda Mitsuyo were compiled into two volumes totaling over 800 pages. The editor of these books Zanun was a childhood friend of Maeda and the two went to the same school in Aomori until Maeda left for Tokyo.

While Maeda no doubt wrote of his experiences in an autobiographical style, Zanun shifted back and forth in the book between Maeda's first-person narrative and a third-person biographical style, occasionally even dramatizing a scene with imagined dialogue. Judging by the length of each section called "fights." Maeda's stories may have been serialized in a newspaper. Those articles were then later collected and published in two volumes in 1912.

A Judo Warrior's Journey Around the Globe Vol. 1	*A Judo Warrior's Journey Around the Globe* Vol.2
1. America [This Book] 2. Britian 3. Belgium and Spain	4. Cuba 5. Mexico 6. Cuba & Guatamala

In the 1950s Zanun published a third volume that summarized the first two books and added additional information regarding Maeda's life in the 1930s up until his death. This translation of Maeda's story will divide each of the two volumes published in 1912 into three sections for a total of six books. The relevant sections from Zanun's later book will be in a seventh book.

The translation will be divided according to the country or region Maeda was challenging local fighters in at that time. One reason for dividing the books is due to the difficulty of the Japanese the authors use, which is different from contemporary Japanese. Following World War Two, the way the Kana syllabary was used changed with some characters being eliminated. Also, the more complex Kanji were simplified, however this book still uses the older Kanji and Kana characters.

In addition, the author and editor use many curious expressions, arcane measurement systems and refer to events that were contemporary to them but are almost 120 years in the past to readers of this translation. Since the goal was to faithfully translate the original text as much as possible, extensive footnotes have been included to help the reader better understand it. The last section of this book will contain contemporary newspaper articles that mention Maeda.

Finally, while readers familiar with Judo will recognize the techniques being described, technical footnotes with current English grappling terms with illustrations have been added. Hopefully, this will help those not familiar with Judo terminology to better visualize the action.

Foreword

Legendary judo master Mitsuyo Maeda is a hazy figure in the history of Brazilian jiu-jitsu. While he is often credited as the instructor of Gracie Jiu-Jitsu founders Carlos and Helio Gracie, little more is said of him in most jiu-jitsu academies. The art's history is mainly the story of the Gracies adapting and improving what they learned from Maeda and using it to win challenge matches. Who Maeda was, what he accomplished, and how that may have influenced the unique blend of Spartan and bushido ideals that the Gracie family champions is not part of the narrative. Fortunately, we have Maeda's own words help us with that.

This book, the first in a series of new translations by Eric Shahan of Mitsuyo Maeda's letters and recollections, begins the story of Maeda and his art before he became the godfather Brazilian jiu-jitsu. In this series, you will travel with the famed judoka through the United States, Europe, and Latin America in the early 20th century as he works to spread judo around the globe. Each volume focuses on his time in a different part of the world. This first volume finds Maeda experiencing the culture shock of living, training, and fighting in America from 1904 to 1907.

What did he experience that was so shocking? Well, there's Maeda and his fellow judoka trying to win converts to judo through kata demonstration but continually being challenged to competitive matches. There's Maeda adapting by posting an open challenge and taking on a series of American wrestlers after opening a dojo. There's Maeda's burning anger at a wrestler who partially blinds one of his judoka friends with illicit strikes in a wrestling match. There's even a scene with Maeda squaring off against multiple opponents in a street brawl and being chased by the cops as he fled the scene.

In short, he experienced many things that parallel the craziness of modern MMA's early years.

How these experiences may have influenced what later became Brazilian jiu-jitsu is a long and involved discussion. Still, readers familiar with both jiu-jitsu and MMA will find some of Maeda's strategies and techniques familiar. For example, Maeda eventually gives up on enticing people to study judo with kata demonstrations alone and asks for challengers at the end of his demos. Then he immediately throws his challenger and applies a joint lock to get it over with quickly. There is also a challenge match where Maeda describes wrapping his legs around a wrestler from behind and choking him unconscious. In fact, Maeda has a few asides where he describes the ways opponents try to win with illicit strikes, groin grabs, scratching, etc. and how to deal with them.

All of the things mentioned above make Maeda's autobiography an important work of martial arts history, but it's also a valuable travelogue. Japan had only been open to the world for about 40 years at the start of Maeda's travels. In fact, his descriptions of being a lone Japanese in Atlanta, Georgia or Selma, Alabama in 1905 may be unique in travel literature. Listening to Maeda use familiar Japanese things (units of measurement, comparisons to well-known Japanese people or places, etc.) to help his original audience visualize his opponents and understand his struggles gives modern readers a very different view of 1905 America. Though Shahan does a good job of helping the modern reader understand these references through copious footnotes, what he delivers is a point of view that's at the crossroads of history. It's a man barely one generation removed from a centuries-old feudal Japanese society trying to make sense of the newness and contradictions of a young America.

In addition to the Japanese language and culture footnotes, Shahan also includes American newspaper clips from the era that mention Maeda. In the appendix, there are reviews of his judo demonstrations, reports on his matches, and even some brief interview excerpts. Taken as a whole, they give some contemporary American perspectives on Maeda's time in the United States and help fill some of the gaps in his narrative.

In short, Eric Shahan has done the heavy work for martial arts or fight sport enthusiasts interested Mitsuyo Maeda's life in America. He has translated the first parts of an autobiographical work largely unavailable to the English-speaking world until now. He has given readers unfamiliar with Japanese language and culture everything they need to understand the cultural lens Maeda saw the America through. Shahan has even given readers the historical American newspaper clips so they don't have to wonder what Americans made of the judo legend. Everything you need to understand the first part of Mitsuyo Maeda's story as he told it is here. The rest will come in subsequent volumes as Shahan translates Maeda's adventures in Europe and Latin America and takes us deeper into the prehistory of Brazilian jiu-jitsu and modern MMA. For now, read on and join a young Maeda as he begins his journey.

Keith Vargo

Tokyo, Japan

August 2022

A JUDO WARRIOR'S JOURNEY AROUND THE GLOBE・世界横行柔道武者修業

MAEDA MITSUYO・前田光世

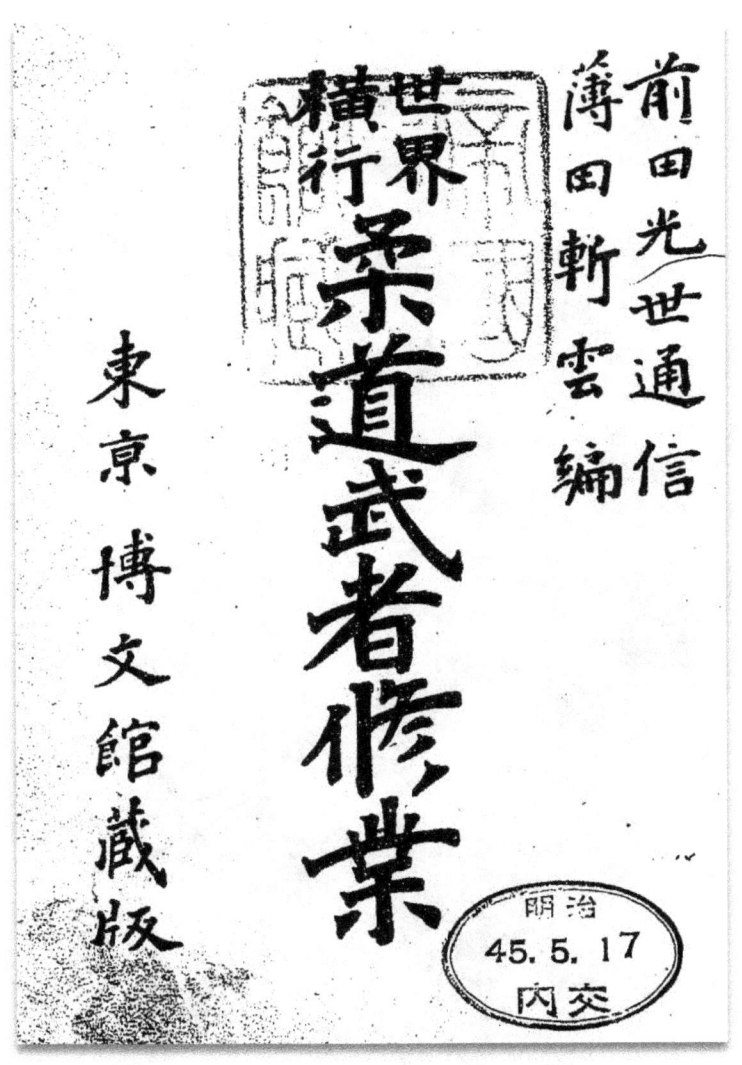

A Judo Warrior's Journey Across the Globe
Volume 1: America 1904 ~ 1907

The Letters of Maeda Mitsuyo (1878 ~ 1941)
Edited by Usuda Zanun (1877 ~ 1956)

MAEDA MITSUYO・前田光世

渡米した頃の富田常次郎(中)と前田光世(左)。

Photograph of Maeda Mitsuyo (left) and Tomita Tsunejiro (center) soon after arriving in America.

A Recent Picture of Maeda Yondan

Note: Yondan (4th degree black belt) has been crossed out and Hachidan (8th degree) written in, though the highest rank he was awarded was Nanadan (7th degree) posthumously in 1941.

MAEDA MITSUYO・前田光世

最近の前田四八段

A Recent Picture of Maeda Yondan

A JUDO WARRIOR'S JOURNEY AROUND THE GLOBE・世界横行柔道武者修業

はしがき

西洋人が體軀巨大で、力量の競爭には、日本人は迚も敵はないと云ふのが、我々一般の考だ。處が日露戰爭に出た軍人に聞いて見ると、愈よ格鬪戰になると、露兵の巨大な體軀などは一向苦にならない、唯だ勇氣が最後の勝利を占める、突いたり斬つたりするには、巨大な體軀の方が的が大きくて具合が好いと云ふ。併しそれは眞劍の場合の事で體術の競技となつたら、是こそは迚も日本人は駄目だらうと思ふて居た。處が此の豫想が全然一掃さるべき例證とし

Introductory Remarks
By Usuda Zanun

"Westerners are giants and Japanese cannot compete with their power" is considered common knowledge in Japan. That being said, when I spoke with veterans of the Russo-Japanese War of 1904-05 and they told me about their experiences with close-quarters combat. One veteran put it like this,

The Russian soldiers were of gigantic proportions so at first it seemed like we would be in for a tough time. However, it turned out that our bravery was the key to victory. When we were stabbing or cutting, those giant bodies make for an easy target.

However, this veteran was referring to Shinken, fighting with bladed weapons. I was sure that if the competition was in Taijutsu, unarmed combat, then Japanese people wouldn't stand a chance. Fortunately, the publication of this book sweeps away that preconceived notion.

はしがき　

本書を提供する時機が來た。五尺三寸餘りの普通の日本人が世界を橫行して、到る處其地の強力者を屈服させ、百戰百勝、大いに國威を發揚して居ると云ふ事は我々の意を強うするに足る。日本人は書生袴を棄てると共に一切の運動を廢して了ふ傾向がある、日本人早老の原因はこゝに在る。本書に依つて見ると、英人などは五十を越へてから柔道擊劍の稽古を始める傾向だ。本書は新代の武者修業記として以外に、空想冒險談と異つた、種々の利益を讀者に與へ得ると信ずる。

明治四十五年五月

編　者　記

A JUDO WARRIOR'S JOURNEY AROUND THE GLOBE・世界横行柔道武者修業

It is the story of a Japanese man of average height travelling across the globe. Standing only 5 Shaku 3 Sun, 160 centimeters, tall he nevertheless submitted the strongest fighters in each place he landed. He took on 100 challengers and won 100 times. A feat that dramatically raised our national prestige and serves to strengthen our resolve.

Japanese have abandoned wearing the scholar's Hakama and, at the same time, there is a tendency in society to completely abandon exercise. Therefore, Japanese are becoming feeble as if we are elderly.

If you read this book, you will see that there is a movement among the English, as well as other foreigners, to begin studying Judo or Gekken (Japanese style fencing) despite being nearly fifty years old or more.

This book serves as a record of intense martial training for the new generation. Unexpectedly, it reads like a fictional adventure story with the difference being the reader can achieve real profit by reading it.

Written in May of Meiji 45 (1912)

世界横行 柔道武者修業

講道館四段 前田光世 通信
薄田斬雲 編

　初陣　

（一）米國 (自三十七年十一月 至四十年二月)

初陣

▲紐育から少し距れたウエスト、ポイントの米國陸軍士官學校では、今日は日本の柔道家が來ると云ふので、早や午刻近い頃、學生教授一同玄關に立って校門外を見渡して居る。『今日來る柔道家と云ふのは何んなだい、又例の贋物ぢやないかね』生徒の一人は疑はしい目をして一同を見廻はした。『若し贋物だつた

A Judo Warrior's Journey Around the Globe: America
November of Meiji 37 to February of Meiji 40 (1904~1907)

The Dispatches of Kodokan Yondan Maeda Mitsuyo (1878~1941)
Edited by Usuda Zanun (1877~1956)

初陣 *Uijin*
First Battle

Not too far from New York City lies West Point, the American Army's officer training school. From early in the morning, students and instructors were all waiting excitedly by the front gate, gazing out. They were waiting for a pair of Judoka from Japan. One student was viewing the scene with suspicion.
"This Judoka[1] that's coming...what kind of person is he? Bet he is one of those charlatans."
Another man whistled and said, "If he's not what he says he is, I'll crush him with one blow and drive the breath from his body." The man was a tall soldier, standing over 6 Shaku[2], 180 centimeters, and he was also very fat. The soldier was a recently commissioned apprentice officer blessed with a massive body like a small mountain weighing 30 Kan[3], 113 kilograms. The soldier was as a football champion and had recently graduated from this school.
Just then another student approached. He also had an impressive physique and seemed to be grinding his teeth before responding to the apprentice officer's disdainful comment.
"With that giant body of yours, he won't give you any trouble. For my part, I will show you how I can stop him in one breath! With all due respect, you are a champion at playing ball, while I am a champion wrestler. If there is to be a duel between Jujutsu and Sumo[4], it is clearly something I should be taking part in." This

---

[1] Judoka 柔道家 a Judo practitioner.
[2] Shaku 尺 is an old unit of measurement. 1 Shaku is 30.3 cm.
[3] Kan 貫 is and old unit of weight. 1 Kan is 3.75 kilograms.
[4] The author refers to wrestling as "Sumo." The Japanese sport Sumo is written 相撲, however wrestling was also referred to as Sumo but with the Kanji 角力 meaning "test of strength" or "comparing strength."

student was the university wrestling champion of the United States.

Another young and distinguished officer said, "Yeah, but if these are some kind of Judo-impostors, letting them take hold of the pure bodies of our students seems highly improper. I will strike them down with one blow of my iron fist and steal their gall bladders."[5]

Another young officer, who had just graduated the previous year, looked thoughtful before turning to the vice-principal and saying, "Sensei, just a thought, but since these Judo practitioners are travelling with Uchida Sadatsuichi, the Japanese Consul General, they probably have a good grounding in Judo. Earlier I saw the colonel, who is standing in as the school representative in place of the principal, set out for the train station by horse-drawn carriage. That shows how much respect they have for these guests."

"According to the introduction given by the Japanese Consul General, several prominent Judoka travelled from Japan to our country at the end of last year, to introduce Judo to America. That is why there are here...ah, They are preparing the welcoming cannon shot, I think the horse-drawn carriage has come into view."

"Well that certainly sounds like they are true-Judoka. What are their names?"

"The head teacher is Tomita Rokudan[6] and the other is named Maeda Yondan."

The students began cheering and exclaiming, "Ah! I can see the horse-drawn carriage!" Then with a *Boom!* the welcoming cannon shot was fired, making everything shake as the horses came through the gates of the school pulling the carriage smartly.

In the front of the carriage was the colonel, who was serving as the school representative in place of the principal, along with two or three officers. Seated calmly in the back, in the positions reserved for distinguished visitors, were the Judoka. In the center was the Japanese Consul General Uchia, on the right was Tomita Rokudan and seated on the left was Maeda Yondan. Maeda was wearing a new jacket and bowler hat and appeared the epitome of a fine

---

[5] Tan wo Ubau 膽を奪う "Steal the gall bladder" means to take away the fighting spirit and causing them to become fearful.

[6] The author refers to Judoka by their last name and rank, in this case Rokudan (6th degree black belt) and Yondan (4th degree black belt.)

gentleman, without a hair out of place.

The students lining the entrance to the school shouted *Banzai!*[7] as they were buffeted by the breeze of the rapidly passing carriage. This was mid-January of Meiji 38, 1905. Late the previous year, on November 16th of Meiji 37, 1904, Mr. Maeda had accompanied Mr. Tomita to America to spread Judo in that land. After three weeks, they arrived in New York.

This was right in the middle of the Russo-Japanese war when our army was winning one victory after another. That these two Judo instructors had journeyed to America right in the middle of this time meant the pair had a certain celebrity status. In America, there was a huge amount of positive feeling with regards to Japan and this was reflected in the considerable interest given to Judo. After arriving in New York, Maeda and company immediately began searching for a way to begin demonstrating and lecturing about Judo. However, their initial efforts were stymied by a lack of language ability in that land. Since they next sought to open a Dojo, it was necessary to seek out a gymnasium or school they could use for lessons.

At the time, a Japanese researcher named Dr. Tanizu was working as an assistant professor of veterinary medicine at Columbia University. Maeda and Tomita approached the professor, and he agreed to be an intermediary and negotiate with the university on behalf of Maeda, for a position as a Judo instructor. The university's response was, "This year is almost at an end. However, we could offer a position in the early spring."

Later, Professor Tanizu successfully negotiated with the Young Men's Christian Association, and the YMCA agreed to offer an acceptable amount of remuneration. The initial class was 80 students which they divided into three groups and had classes twice a day, once in the morning and once in the afternoon. Maeda and Tomita took turns teaching three times a week.

Since this situation was set to continue for the foreseeable future, the pair decided to practice conversation. While they worked on their language skills, the 37th year of Meiji became the 38th year.

---

[7] It is possible the students shouted *Banzai!* "ten-thousand years!" (as opposed to an English greeting like "hurrah!") since the word was known at the time, particularly after the Russo-Japanese war.

And once again in the new year, news of a grand victory in the Russo-Japanese War was reported. Since Americans at the time were very supportive of Japan, whenever Maeda and Tomita were walking around town the local children would shout *Nippon Banzai!* as they walked by, before jumping up and swinging from their arms. Japanese people living in the United States at the time found themselves quite unexpectedly at the center of attention.

At the same time, the topic of Japanese Judo began to spring up amongst average Americans. Unfortunately, a certain element amongst Japanese living in America took this as an opportunity. These villains claimed, "I am a Judo champion! The reason the Japanese soldiers were able to overcome the giant Russian soldiers was because they knew the secret of Judo." There were many who used wild exaggerations[8] such as this to make money, despite being complete beginners.

Around this time, Maeda saw an advertisement for a Judo correspondence school in the newspaper. The book for sale was one with photographs of Judo Kata accompanied by an explanation. Though it seemed to contain little more than a dollar's worth of information, copies were flying out for 10 or even 15 dollars. At any rate, the ad was very self-assured. Americans were apparently quite familiar with the author, who shall remain unnamed, as an expert in Japanese Judo.

Maeda and Tomita eventually figured out that he was "Great Sensei" So-and-so. However, they had never heard of this Great Sensei before. They supposed he may have been an old practitioner of Shinyo Ryu.[9] When they looked at the book however, it was not an elderly Sensei, but a picture of a young man. This realization could not help but irritate Maeda who decided to find out exactly who this "Great Sensei" was. So, he looked up the address of the Judo correspondence school and went to pay the Great Sensei a

---

[8] O-Hora Fuki 大法螺吹き "Blowing a great conch shell trumpet" meaning to brag or exaggerate wildly.

[9] Referring to Tenjin Shinyo Ryu 天神真楊流 "Divine True Willow School." This school of Jujutsu was founded in the 1830s by Iso Mataemon 磯又右衛門.

visit.[10]

When Maeda finally succeeded in meeting him, however, there was a man with not the slightest whiff of "martial artist" about him. He had a curious face, and his clothes were of the latest fashion. At a glance, Maeda read him as an American scoundrel, but asked politely, "May I inquire where you studied Judo?"

The Great Sensei smirked and answered condescendingly, "I have never done anything as unsophisticated as training in Judo." Seeming to consider Maeda a young lad, he opened his mouth wide and, quite without shame, added in a loud voice, "Young man."

Standing before this charlatan "Great Sensei" who was completely without shame, Maeda was fuming. However, the man looked like he was ready to spring one lie after another. Seeing that this wasn't the time or place to launch himself violently at the man, Maeda decided to change his approach.

---

[10] This may have been the advertisement. *The American College of Physical Culture and Jiu-jitsu* was run by John F. McDonald. He apparently learned the techniques from John O'Brian, who previously lived in Nagasaki, Japan and taught President Roosevelt for 2 months in 1902.

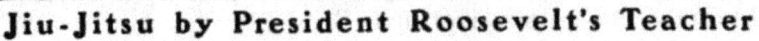

"You certainly have made a name for yourself with this book, may I asked how you were able to write this guide?"

Having been pressed for an answer the Great Sensei expounded casually, "You probably won't understand how we do things in America." While puffing on a cigar he added, "I have never seen Judo before, however a friend of mind knows a little about Shinyo Ryu Kata. I talked with him about those Kata and took some photographs. Then I added some explanation. For example, *As the picture above shows, step forward with your right foot to your enemy's right side. At the same time pull the left hand...*and so on. I can crank out a book like that in no time!"

The Great Sensei's off the cuff manner astounded Maeda and he cleared his throat and replied, "If you come and watch one of my lectures on Judo, and see what a person with actual knowledge can do, you may end up being at a loss for words. I don't do any sort of tricks or sleight of hand. Be that as it may, I must say that I am impressed with your way of doing things. However, no matter how adept a person or Sensei may be at Judo, the Japanese martial arts that are part of Bushido should not be advertised as products. Though I must take into consideration Americans and the way Americans do things, I don't think this will lead to your success. I firmly believe this. Americans are quick to consume any rare thing they come across and recently the newspapers writers are all scribbling in unison praising Japan."

Maeda continued, "Judo is a technique developed by Japan that has no equivalent elsewhere in the world. The newspapers are going on and on writing that Judo is a "secret technique" or arguing it is a "magic technique," or saying, "Judo had a hand in the recent military victories." And, just as you might expect, in less than half a year, the other side has begun to write slanderous articles. To me this all sounds like squawking gossip done by overbearing wives in the alleys between houses. To be frank, I feel I should use this chance to consider the course of action me and my compatriots will take. Should we just do as we please, adopting that great mindset your ilk have, with no concern for what others may think? I deeply admire you, after all this is America, not Japan. We have no choice other than to drink in the culture and traditions of this land."

Through this effusive speech, which calculated the complex ins-and-outs of succeeding in this land, Maeda was able to craft the first page in his plan. He could only laugh ironically at this situation. This Judo correspondence school had succeeded by using deft theatrics in their advertisements.

Another example of how Judo was being presented was a newspaper article that stated in an exaggerated fashion, "Last night at such-and-such-a-place a ruffian acted in an untoward manner with a young lass. However, the young lass was versed in the secret techniques of Judo and was able to crush the villain." The accompanying illustration showed a girl of 17 or 18 submitting a giant villain who stood, 180 centimeters, by using an arm breaking technique.

Another example is, "Near San Francisco, a giant man threatened a housewife, however the woman became enraged and used Judo on the man, throwing him 4 or 5 Ken,[11] 7 ~ 9 meters." The article grossly exaggerated the situation to the point it became a society story. However, this is what the Judo correspondence school bet their money on and placed ads in newspapers accordingly. It is so divorced from reality to almost be a Kyogen, comical story.

So, the current state of affairs of Judo in America was: though Japanese Judo was held in high regard, there were very few people who had actually seen it. At the same time there was nobody not talking about Judo. Into this situation came prospectors, looking to make their fortune. At first this might seem to be a disadvantage to Maeda and company; however, it meant that most Americans were aware of Judo. Thus, since Maeda and company were true Judoka, they were like pioneers. There was an opportunity here for Maeda and company if only they could find a way to make it happen. And thus far, it had eluded them.

On the other hand, there were the Japanese vagabonds seeking adventure. They went about bragging, "I am a true Japanese Judoka! I will challenge any boxer or wrestler in America who wants to come forward!" Though they talked big, making broad declarations saying they would "fight at the drop of a hat," they didn't have much training to speak of. This meant that they were flattened by strong American fighters leaving them shamed. These sorts of people were the first obstacle Maeda and company had to overcome.

---

[11] A Ken 間 is equivalent to 6 Shaku, or 180 centimeters.

美人難 *Bijin-nan*
Trouble With a Beautiful Girl

So, the situation was, Americans' passion for Japanese Judo was heating up and, at the same time, rascals from our own country in America were unfurling great banners claiming, "We are true Japanese Judoka," but then frequently failing spectacularly.

Thus, Maeda and company, our countrymen and true Japanese Judoka sought to distance themselves from the other group. While they were fretting over various approaches, they got a lucky break. Our Japanese Council General, Mr. Uchida, invited Maeda and Tomita to travel from New York to West Point, the American Army Officer training school to give a lecture and demonstration of Judo.

Thus, as was written on the first page of this book, Tomita and Maeda were met at the train station by officials from the school, climbed aboard a horse-drawn carriage around noon on the day in question and headed for West Point. They passed through the gates of the school and were greeted by several ceremonial cannon blasts as the students and teachers cheered their arrival.

They arrived at the school just past noon. Maeda and company were first escorted by the man who had picked them up at the train station, Colonel So-and-so who was serving as the school representative in place of the principal, to his house for lunch.

However, as it turned out when seated at the table for lunch, Maeda was placed beside the Colonel's young daughter. She had a graceful face and she was sparkling in her Sunday-best dress. Her lips were a pale red and she gazed at Maeda with deep insightful eyes as she spoke. For his part, Maeda couldn't understand a word she said and was only able to respond with *YES!* or *NO!* However, since he answered her questions with *Yes! Yes!* the young girl with the lovely face continued. She looked Maeda directly in the eyes and commented, "I've heard your country has beautiful scenery?"
Yes!
"There is a mountain called Fuji there, right?"
Yes!

So, despite being the guest of honor at an official dinner a dark cloud was spreading as Maeda broke out in a sweat as he continued to repeat *Yes!* He had not, as yet, touched his knife and fork.

"You should try some of the food" she said.
Maeda replied *Yes!* but his hands remained fixed where they were.
"Oh dear, you aren't eating anything, does the food does not agree with you?"
Oh, ye-s ye-s!

From that point on the young girl must have sensed something and she did not really talk to him much after that. Maeda breathed a sigh of relief.

Eventually the lunch ended, and Maeda was able to escape from the *Ye-s, Ye-s* beauty. The colonel took them on a tour of the school, showing them the classrooms before leading them up to the lecture hall on the second floor, where they could begin their lecture and demonstration. Of course, all the students as well as all the teachers were in attendance, lining both sides of the room, staring with almost feverish eyes at Maeda and Tomita. After changing into their Keikogi[12], Maeda and Tomita advanced powerfully into the center of the training space.

Upon seeing this unexpected pair, the students exchanged glances with each other before smirking and giggling, saying, "These tiny fellows travelled from a far-off land 3000 Ri,[13] 11,700 kilometers, across the ocean to test their skill against us? A country whose people developed into physically powerful people? My sides are hurting with laughter."

---

[12] Keikogi 稽古着 Judo training uniform.
[13] Ri 里 is an archaic unit of distance equivalent to 3.9 kilometers.

白袴時代 *Shirohakama Jidai*
White Hakama Era

The fact that the student's side was hurting from scornful laughter was not without reason. When Maeda was training at the Kodokan, he was not considered small. However, when compared to the American students at the officer training school and their tall, well-developed bodies, all of whom stood 6 Shaku, 180 centimeters, tall, the Japanese Judoka seemed wretchedly tiny in comparison. Maeda stood 5 Shaku 4 Sun, 162 cm, and weighted 18 Kan, 68 kg. Tomita was even shorter and weighted less. If these two could throw the officers in training everyone would have to admit the newspaper articles stating that Japanese Judo was in fact magic were true.

Maeda was born in Nakatsugaru District of Aomori Prefecture. He turns 32 this year.[14] His father was a friendly, outgoing man and his mother was a strong woman who was fresh and vibrant as split bamboo.[15] Their son Maeda seemed to have inherited half his personality from each parent. Around the time Maeda graduated from upper elementary school,[16] there were quite a few rumors about his strength, along the lines of, "Maeda can carry two bales of rice, one on each shoulder![17]"

When he went in for a check-up the school doctor said he was fully developed with a solid frame and good musculature. He complimented the youth by saying, "If you became a Sumo wrestler, with that body you would no doubt be top class!"

Maeda first began studying Judo when he travelled to Tokyo to enroll in Waseda High School. This was most likely in Meiji 31, 1898. At the time Waseda Technical School had set up a Dojo and Judo was being taught there. Around that time, 5 or 6 students from

---

[14] This book was published in 1912.

[15] While bamboo is very durable, if cut vertically it splits in half cleanly. The outside is green and fresh and the inside is white and has a satisfyingly straight cut.

[16] Part of the old Japanese school system. Students attended from 10 ~ 14 years old.

[17] One bale of rice weighs 60 kilograms.

the neighboring Waseda High School went to the Technical School to train. Maeda was one of those boys.

The first Judo instructor invited to teach at Waseda was Shodan[18] Kawahara Yataro of the Kodokan. Next was Iwazaki Shodan, Washio Shodan, and finally Isoya Nidan. Amongst these teachers, Iwazaki Shodan had trained the longest and was the most passionate about teaching. The man that taught Maeda the basics of Judo was Iwazaki Shodan.

Other people you could see at the Dojo around this time were Oki Teisuke, who recently passed away, Inoue Masaji and others. The members with whom Maeda had a good relationship later became part of what is now called the Tengu "Mountain Goblin[19]" University Sports Appreciation Society. His friends were the head of the University Sports Appreciation Society Oshikawa Shunro and the head of the Baseball division Kiyo.

Eventually Maeda transferred to the Waseda Technical School and began training at the Kodokan, later becoming one of the top Judoka. After training at the Kodokan for about a year, he became Shodan.

So, by November of Meiji 37, 1904, when he accompanied Tomita Rokudan to America, he had become Yondan and was one of the most powerful Judo wrestlers at the Kodokan. At the time there were many powerful figures such as Satake, Itoh, Samura, Handa, Yamada, Ohno, Iai and other great masters of this art. Men such as Adachi, Nagaoka, Uchida, Tomita, Yamashita and Yokoyama did not train actively but served as advisors. Mifune and Toku came somewhat after this era.

---

[18] The book notes the ranks mentioned were the ranks "at that time."
[19] Tengu 天狗 are a kind of supernatural creature that lives in the mountains of Japan. It can take many humanoid forms, though often with exaggerated features, like the face of a crow. While considered tricksters, they also are known to teach martial arts.

第一勝 *Dai Issho*
First Victory

晴れの場 *Hare no Ba*
Debut

So, at long last it was time to introduce Judo to the students at the officer's training school. First, they showed Kata, introducing over a hundred techniques including Nage-no-Kata, Koshiki-no-Kata, Ju-no-Kata, Taiso-no-Kata and Shobu-no-Kata. Tomita served as the Tori and Maeda was the Uke. In other words, Maeda's role as the one receiving the techniques was to be thrown over a hundred times. The person who is receiving the technique needs to be good, more so than the person applying the technique, otherwise the Waza will not be clear to the observer. Maeda was used to the firm Japanese Tatami mats that covered the floor of the Kodokan, however here the mats were soft and more like Futon blankets than mats. Thus, it was quite difficult to take Ukemi, breakfalls and rolls, on these mats. He was as careful as possible, but it felt as if his bones were going to break and his body hurt all over.

However, as it turned out, though Maeda had endured the long demonstration, the 100 Kata they showed seemed to leave no impression on the observers. Later, when taking volunteers to do Randori, they couldn't quite replicate what was shown in the demonstration. Thus, scornful comments like, "For the demonstration they planned the whole thing out. You can't really do a huge throw like that in real-life, it's all some kind of acrobatics show!" And so on and so forth.

Rather than faithfully demonstrating the Kata one after another, they should have showed some techniques from Nage-no-Kata five or six times and then immediately called for volunteers to do Randori, free sparring with the goal of applying that technique. Then they could have explained the finer points of each technique. Later, they could have continued in order and introduced the Koshiki-no-Kata and the Taiso-no-Kata and saved themselves a lot of effort and succeeded in their quest. Today however, was Maeda and company's first foray after arriving in America. Their debut went a little too far.

Having finished demonstrating Kata, it was now time for Maeda to train with some of the students as partners. Though Maeda intended for the next phase of the demonstration to be training, the students were only interesting in dueling. The students came at him full force with their huge bodies and Maeda was worried he might injure a student, so he demurred. However, it seemed he was expected to throw his opponent in some fashion and then use a Gyaku, joint lock, to make them submit in a manner that left no doubt who the winner was. As it turned out, the initial explanation of their plan amounted to nothing.

If you don't start off by saying, "This is what Judo is all about" no matter what you say afterward, it won't compute. On the other hand, if you start off explaining carefully and slowly, you will end up with a response like, "Judo is more difficult than I expected, I wasn't able to do anything." This means you will end up leaving a bad impression and everyone will be muttering their dissatisfaction like a Tengu mountain goblin.[20] Confusing people over what Judo

---

[20] Tengu 天狗 Are supernatural creatures with a long history in Japan. Originally referring to a celestial event, like comets in the sky, they later evolved into trickster creatures who waylaid errant Buddhist monks. They became associated with martial arts and stories of famous Samurai who were secretly taught by Tengu abound. They generally appear humanoid though with a long nose or an avian head. The illustration, below, is from an Edo Era document that contains drawings of two different kind of Tengu demonstrating techniques.

is will lead to such comments and those comments will, in turn, leap right over to the newspapers. They will feature a distorted version of the events, concluding, "Japanese Judo is of no value!" Once this begins it will not be easy to bring public sentiment back.

So, Maeda's first opponent turned out to be the man introduced in the first section of this book, the American-style wrestling champion. He possessed a splendid body and, he was clearly a student, not possessing the sly manner of a man that wrestles for money. The student charged right at Maeda, intending to crush him. However, the wrestler gave Maeda exactly what he wanted. Maeda seized the man's sleeves, shoved his hips in deep and used that set up to hurl the student's giant body into the air. The student's feet rotated up towards the ceiling as he flipped completely over.

The wrestler got up immediately, looking frustrated, and charged in again like a warrior. Maeda slipped his right hand deep under the student's armpit and launched him with a perfect textbook Koshi Nage, hip throw. Again, the student rose, and Maeda proceeded to topple him again with Okuri Ashi-barai, foot sweep. After Maeda had thrown him five or six times, the student became cautious, lowering his hips and putting power in his extended arms.

Next, Maeda made a show of yanking the student back, before shoving forward with a *Un!* The opponent, after staggering when being pushed, became panicked and thrust forward with all his strength. Maeda used this chance to plant his right foot on his opponent's lower abdomen and set up for a Sutemi Waza, sacrifice throw. Maeda pulled the student's arms in, and with that as the center threw him in a great half circle so he slammed into the ground with a *Doshin!* sound.[21]

---

[21] The Japanese language has a lot of sound words. For example, *Doshin!* is the sound of something hitting the floor hard.

Maeda immediately mounted him and applied a Kuzure Kesa Gatame, Choking with Your Arms Like a Broken Monk's Vestment.[22] However, the American wrestling champ didn't submit so easily, and managed to roll on top of Maeda. In response, Maeda reached up and grabbed the collar of his shirt with both hands and started to pull the wrestler down in a choke. Suddenly all the spectators began cheering and clapping. Maeda had no idea what was going on. "Maybe seeing this kind of choke, they feel the bout is over?"

So, he stood up and rejoined the duel with his opponent. Seizing the student, Maeda threw him down hard and then immediately took hold of his arm in a joint-lock, causing him to yield. Later when he thought about the scene, Maeda realized when he was on his back, the applause from the audience was because in American-style wrestling pinning the back to the Tatami mats means defeat.

Maeda, having finished training, went back to the changing room for a break. When he later returned to the training and lecture hall, he was surprised to see Tomita Rokudan engaged in a debate with two giant men, the officer trainee, and the recently commissioned officer, who were insisting on a duel with Tomita. From the beginning, Tomita had not intended to train or engage in duels with the students, however they were quite insistent. Maeda was worried about prolonging this debate, considering both where they were and what they were trying to accomplish. The fact that both lacked fluency in English compounded the problem.

---

[22] Kuzushi Kesa Katame 崩袈裟固 from *How to Become Expert at Judo* 柔道上達法 1939.

〔固 袈 裟 崩〕

冨田六段の大奮闘 *Tomita Rokudan no Daifuntoh*
The Great Struggle of Tomita Rokudan

The two giant men, the officer and the officer in training, were adamant about training with Tomita. The way they saw things was since Maeda was the one getting bounced all over the room by Tomita's throws, Tomita must be an instructor several ranks higher than Maeda. Further, since Tomita was much smaller of stature, they figured that, no matter how great a Sensei he was, his body was only half the size of theirs so they could crush him in one move. Clearly, the pair was reveling in their plan, and it seemed that the situation could not be resolved without agreeing to their request. Tomita replied with, "Very well, I shall do as you request."

First up was the officer, who shook hands with Tomita before dropping into a stance. The officer immediately charged straight at Tomita with great intensity. Tomita, for his part, made use of that power and grabbed both his sleeves, before yanking back. This caused the officer to lose his balance and crash down on the mats with both knees and he didn't get back up. He had injured his knees and couldn't rise. The match ended with the officer borrowing the shoulders of two of his fellows to make his way off the mats. Maeda found out later that this officer had previously injured his knees while falling off a horse, and this caused the same injury to rebound.

Next was the officer in training. He had just graduated from West Point the previous year and he was full of vim and vigor. A tall, fat soldier who used to be a football champion, he weighed 250 Kin[23] or 30 Kan, 150 kilograms, more than double Tomita. The duel began and Tomita noticed right away his opponent moved like a rat. Based on his footwork and body stance, Tomita speculated he had likely seen Judo at some point. Seeing how he moved, he may have even trained in Judo to a degree. He did no try to charge in like a half-warrior, half-wild boar as the previous opponent did and he did not allow Tomita to take hold of his Keikogi. Both combatants kept their breathing measured as they glared at each other, closing the distance with a Jiri-jiri sound of carefully advancing. Both were on

---

[23] Kin 斤 is an archaic unit of weight equivalent to 0.6 Kilograms. It is not clear why he gives the man's weight in both Kin and Kan.

their guard. As one person closed in, the other retreated. When one retreated, the other advanced. Though Tomita had refined his technique over decades, he was not going to try and leap in and strike a Kyusho, vital point, and kill his opponent. However, he also couldn't pretend this was regular training and strike lightly against a giant man who was a fierce football champion twice his size.

However, the giant man didn't seem inclined to close the distance of his own volition. If pressed, he withdrew if Tomita withdrew, the giant advanced. Overall, his strategy was very well-defined. If you were to compare the two, it was as if an adult was facing off against a youth of 14 or 15 years. Truly it was a curious spectacle, and Maeda's palms were wet with sweat as he gripped them into fists. As he watched, Tomita must have seen an opening because he leapt in like a bird and seized the giant's sleeves, before setting up for his specialty, Tomoe-Nage. However, his opponent was a tall, fat soldier weighing 30 Kan, and he was knowledgeable in how to defend against this type of attack. The giant put power in his lower abdomen and arched his back, resisting Tomita's pull.

Though Tomita had applied his technique expertly, it didn't lead to success. The giant then hoisted his Japanese opponent up in the air. With a *Ha!* the giant threw the tiny soldier Tomita with all his might across the mats as if he were a football.

However, Tomita's body was nothing at all like a ball and due to his years of intensive training in Judo, the techniques were part of his very soul. Though he was thrown 2 Ken, 3.6 meters, he stood up and calmly faced his opponent. Unsurprisingly, the giant man's eyes went wide and he appeared stunned.

Eventually, Tomita found another opening and again whipped in and tried to apply Tomoe Nage again. This time was different, and he got the giant 30 Kan man off the ground on his skinny leg, and breathed out as he yanked hard on both his sleeves. Just as Tomita was about to launch the man over his head and flip him over his head in a textbook throw, his power fell short. The giant man extended his arms like a turtle and wobbled there, struggling hard to save himself at the last moment. With a grunt of *Un!* he arched his back and put power in his lower abdomen before hoisting Tomita up in the air. However, Tomita wasn't going to get caught by the same trick twice, and with a jerk twisted himself out of the man's grip and faced him again.

The officer in training was in shock by his narrow escape and a killing fury appeared on his face. He charged directly in and grabbed both of Tomita's shoulders, holding fast like an eagle gripping its prey. Then relying solely on strength, he began to swing Tomita, who was a head shorter, around by his shoulders. Tomita was being handled like a toy and his feet came 1 Shaku, 30 cm, off the mats. The man swung him around and he fluttered like the flame of a lantern in the breeze and, if the giant man had had a bit of knowledge, he would have done a Sutemi to the side while slinging his opponent with all his might. If he had done so, Tomita would have been thrown in a jumble all the way across the room. Maeda was paralyzed with tension while watching. At the same time the muscles in the forehead of Uchida, the Japanese consul general forehead seemed to be spasming of their own accord.

However, the giant didn't possess the knowledge or expertise to hit on such a solution. So, he continued to swing Tomita around until, exhaustion spreading on his face, he released his grip. Once released, Tomita dropped down as if he was leaping off a horse, and without the slightest effort rolled lightly to his feet. Maeda breathed a sigh of relief.

Next, Tomita was able to read the giant's gambit and he leapt in deep below his chest, looking to apply a Koshi Waza or Ashi Waza. He managed to wrap up one of the giant's legs and was on the verge of toppling him like a big Japanese folding screen. From where he was seated, Maeda could see Tomita had scooped up his opponent's leg. However, this posed no problem for the giant and he didn't wobble. The enemy was a football champion and during games he often stood on one leg while carrying the ball. From behind, he slipped both arms under Tomita's armpits and gripped the smaller man tightly. It was like when the Samurai Noritsune grabbed Yoshitsune at The Battle of Yashima.[24]

---

[24] The Battle of Yashima 屋島の戦い was fought in 1185. Noritsune boarded Yoshistune's boat seeking to capture him but Yoshitsune escaped by leaping away in what is known as 義経八艘飛 or *Yoshitsune*'s Leap over Eight Boats. Now trapped on an enemy ship Noritsune seized two enemy Samurai and leapt into the water, causing all three to sink to their deaths.

However, Tomita Rokudan was channeling Yoshitsune and he was able to wrest free by pushing down with both arms and pulling his head in. Like a fleeing rabbit he leaped away from the source of danger and stood up facing his opponent again, without a hair out of place and still holding his gentlemanly bearing. Compared to the intense training at the Kodokan, this was nothing. Then the giant asked for the "match" to be called, despite the original intent of today being training. At any rate, Tomita and the man shook hands and left it at that.

And that is how the lecture and demonstration ended. The two braves were accompanied by Uchida General Consul back to New York, where they ate dinner and collapsed into bed, exhausted.

They woke up earlier than usual the next day and as they went to the cafeteria of their lodging house there were several customers talking excitedly. They were standing over a table with that morning's newspaper on top. Maeda approached wondering what was going on and a gentleman he had become familiar with indicated the newspaper and said with a smirk, "Look at this! You guys are in the paper!" With his heart pounding Maeda reached for the paper, then stared in disbelief.

The first thing he saw was an illustration of a tiny Japanese man wearing a Kimono and walking with a cane while wrapped in a bandage from his head down to his arm. The title of the article was "Yesterday at West Point, Japan's number one Judoka Tomita Rokudan, was tumbled about by a football champion from that school during a bout." Maeda couldn't move his mouth when he read this.

Yesterday during training Tomita had made a good showing against a giant opponent and, despite not achieving a win, handled him adroitly. And his opponent, despite being twice the size and strength of Tomita had been unable to obtain a victory. Indeed, the giant had been the one to request a stop to the match and it goes without saying that the one who requested the stop should be considered the loser. This newspaper article was 60% fabrication and the remaining 40% of the article reversed the two sides of the duel. The article continued with absurd statements like, "Mr. Tomita was injured and is now in the hospital" which was completely divorced from reality.

It was Tomita who had yanked the officer's sleeves and caused him to come crashing to the ground, thereby injuring his knees. Saying that it was Tomita who was hospitalized as a result of the duel and not the officer cannot be considered an error, it was intentional slander. Clearly this was dog-shit revenge.[25] Clearly the reporter had colluded with the school when writing this article. Such cowardly actions were beyond contempt.

However, at that point Maeda and company were still new and were under the impression that "we are all brothers across the four seas.[26]" They were very straightforward, so they responded with a dry laugh, "What is this?! We could tell them the truth, there were over a hundred pairs of American eyes on us the whole time! However, this sort of false reporting is typically how American news sources operate."

A person who didn't know the truth would be shocked that a famous practitioner of Japanese Judo had been defeated. In fact, word of Tomita's "great defeat" was even reported in Japan. Of course, there was no mention of the way Maeda had freely manipulated the American wrestling champ. All they did was make an amateurish report about how Maeda had been thrown a lot. "The first Japanese man was thrown about like a ball and then Japan's top Judoka Tomita got handled by the football champion." The article continued on in that stunningly deprecating fashion. Even today Maeda is dismayed at the number of Japanese people who think he racked up a huge loss in this encounter. So, to all my Japanese compatriots, sweep aside the falsehoods and understand that against that size opponent with that level of strength, Tomita performed quite admirably.

---

[25] *Inu no kuso de Kataki wo Toru* 犬糞的復讐 Is becoming obsessed with getting revenge for a small slight.

[26] The "four seas" refers to how Japan is surrounded in all directions by ocean, so it refers to "all of Japan." However in this case it is referring to "the whole world." Another translation could be "Think well of all men."

雁柔道大先生 *Gan Judo Dai Sensei*
The Fake Great Judo Sensei

Due to intentional false reporting of their demonstration and lecture at West Point, the American Army officer training school, Maeda and Tomita found that the reputation of Japanese Judo had fallen. Thus, immediately afterward, in a certain New York newspaper a suspicious fellow wrote an article stating, "I am the only true Japanese Judoka!"

He continued unabashedly, going so far as to issue a challenge in the newspaper, "The so-called Judoka who were defeated the other day at West Point Officer training school, were not professional Judo practitioners. They may have trained in Judo a little bit while in school but they are still wet behind the ears. I am a true champion of Japanese Judo, the best in Japan. I am happy to accept a challenge from any person!"

Amazingly an American answered that challenge with an equally belligerent article in the same paper stating his desire for a duel. Passion for Judo had reached a peak at this time, and society was riveted by the unfolding spectacle. The Japanese man then wrote an article that featured his picture and an obviously fictious resume. He then proceeded to explain how Gyakute, wrist locks, are used in Judo in an overly long and rambling manner that bore no basis in reality. The American then responded in kind, bragging about his strength, and talking about how a once-in-a-lifetime duel between American and Japanese fighters would take place the next day. However, while the argument continued back and forth on the front page of the paper, the date of the duel always seemed just out of reach. Public interest in this bout was very high, much to the chagrin of Maeda and Tomita, who actually were true Judoka.

Eventually, Maeda and company couldn't take it anymore and wrote letter after letter to the newspaper company challenging both the American and the Japanese fighter to a duel. However, no matter how many times he wrote, the challenge was never run in the newspaper. All the Japanese residing in New York were firmly on the side of the Judoka and they discussed him incessantly. Maeda and Tomita found the situation intolerable but as it couldn't be helped, they sat on their hands and waited. In his state of irritation, if he had come across that Japanese fellow, Maeda would have thrown him down hard and choked the breath out of him. Maeda also decided that on the day of the match, he would leap in and submit them both before the public. However, the two would-be combatants only continued their duel on the pages of the paper.

January turned to February and Maeda began travelling to Princeton University to teach Judo. During this time the duel between the self-proclaimed Great Japanese Judo Sensei and the American seemed to be on the verge of taking place. One day a Japanese man came to visit Maeda in his hotel. He begged in a lowly manner, "I am a friend of the Judoka you have been reading about, the truth is he is a bit uncertain about this upcoming duel and, I realize this is asking a lot, but he would like to know if you, sir, would take his place in the duel."

Maeda didn't hold back. "I previously sent several letters addressed to your newspaper company, answering the challenges of both parties. However, your paper never once posted them. Further, the man used his position as a Japanese person to declare that we were still wet behind the ears and incapable of anything and your newspaper eagerly published his disgraceful lie. So then, before we talk about me standing in for that man, first I want to meet with that man as well as the American in the same place. If you want me to fight, then my demands have to be met. That is my proposal... however, I must know, did the Great Japanese Judoka ask you to come here? Is he in agreement?"

In response the man twisted his neck and said, "Actually, no. We haven't really discussed it." He then added, "The truth is, with regards to the planned duel, with my friend isn't really such a reliable person, however he has become part of an American show business group and they are managing things. Recently our paper has lost a lot of money. The show business group purchased our paper and, to drive up circulation, they made both parties get into a fiery debate. This drew a lot of interest from the public. Neither I nor my friend have any knowledge of Judo techniques. However, since there was money to be made, he wrote inconsiderate things about you and treated you quite shabbily."

He continued, "Though we saw the challenge you wrote, the newspaper had no intention of running it, since they were interested in entertainment, specifically outrageous stories."

"Now I understand!" replied Maeda.

The man continued, "The fact of the matter is, I know he has no Judo ability, so I have been extremely worried. The loser here is the honor of Japanese Judo. For those of us who are Japanese, honor means everything. I have been fretting about this by myself for some time and decided to pay you a call today to discuss the matter..."

"I understand, I understand!" replied Maeda. For the first time the entire situation became clear. He gave the man his thoughts, "I can see you have spent a long time concerning yourself about Judo and the reputation of Japanese in America. Ask your friend to reconsider what he is doing and join you on the same path, and you can both start again. Please ask your friend if he would like to discuss this with me further."

Receiving such a reply after the paper had spoken of Maeda in such inconsiderate terms, the man could only reply, "Then that is what I shall do." With that he left.

Maeda thought that if the two men came, he would be able to force them into an agreement on his terms and so he waited, but there was no word from the pair.

At this point it would have been hard for Maeda to press a call on either the Japanese man or the man he represented. It is likely they were even now exchanging the agreement form to be signed by both parties for the Japanese-American duel, so it would be difficult to change the arrangement. Further, it wasn't clear how the duel was going to proceed, and since it was based on the desire for a spectacle, no doubt the Japanese man had conspired with the American. They were betting money on this after all and they were no doubt making sure they made money no matter who won or lost.

Eventually, the day of the Japanese-American bout arrived, and the long-awaited match was actually going to go forward. In the first round the American wrestler opened with a hip toss and then leg sweeps, however when compared to Japanese Judo, these were kindergarten-level, and were wholly ineffective. It seemed the Japanese Judoka was thinking "This guy will be an easy match" and tried Maki-komi several times.[27] However, while Maki-komi is a technique favored by Judoka, it turns out, from the perspective of an American wrestler, using such a technique places you on the doorstep of death. Even if a Judoka is an expert at applying this technique, against an American wrestler it is absolutely forbidden. Further, this Japanese man was of meager skill, so the American pinned him to the ground and rendered the Japanese man unable to move. The first round was a glorious defeat for Japanese Judo.

In the second round, the Japanese man planted his right foot on the American's lower abdomen and went for a Tomoe Nage. The throw was good and the American flew over his head. As the man rotated around it seemed as if he was going to slam ingloriously into the mats, however the American rolled expertly and was right back on his feet, hardly making contact with the mats. At this point the Japanese side claimed this as a victory, however the numerous American spectators exploded with derisive cries, silencing the other side's claims. Very well then, after throwing, the American's shoulders have to be touching the mat and if he is not held there, then he can't be declared defeated. The fact that it was the American who was the first to return to a standing position after the Tomoe Nage was testament to the fact that the throw did not result in a

---

[27] Judo techniques from from an early 20th century guide to Kodokan Judo.

Maki-komi

Tomoe Nage

victory.

Since he had been thrown once by Tomoe Nage, the American was on guard against it. He pushed his hips back and down while he firmly gripped the Japanese man's Keikogi. It almost looked like he was crawling his defensive stance was so low, while the Japanese Judoka gripped his opponent's collar. It wasn't clear if both men were just timing their breathing, or if they were glaring at each other or if they were afraid. At any rate, neither made a move and they appeared to be evenly matched and deadlocked. It felt like they were in that position for an hour. The American spectators, who are inherently prone to lobbing insults, were hardly quiet during this time, "What is this cowardly stuff! Are you alive or are you already dead?! Referee! Watch them!" and "Just look at these shitheads glaring at each other for an hour! What's the point?! Oi! Japan's number one Judoka, do you have any breath left in you?" and "What a bunch of fakers, you filthy lying Judoka, you are nothing but a useless monkey!" That and other shouts of derision rained down from every corner of the crowd which was in a total uproar.

Then in the middle of this the American wrestler started to rise up and the Japanese Judoka used that opening to try Tomoe Nage again. However, it didn't go well, and the American was able to roll his body slightly to the side avoiding the throw. From there the American was able to lock up the Judoka. Since it was "best of three" the Japanese man was defeated. The next day, Maeda and Tomita could barely stand to read the disparaging way Japanese Judo was described in the newspaper.

The conditions of the duel were that both parties had to wear Keikogi, that joint locks were banned and that only throws, chokes and pins could be used. For throws, if both shoulders of the person being thrown touched the mats, then it counted as a fall.[28] When suppressing, if both shoulders touched the mats, it was a win. For chokes, it would only count as a win if the opponent signaled defeat. For a Judoka these are not particularly difficult conditions. What Maeda learned form this is that one opponent pushing until the other concedes is the safest bet.

When it was all said and done, the newspapers were united in

---

[28] In this case, fall refers to the ending of a match.

their description of how "The Number One Japanese Judoka" was defeated by "Our American Wrestler." They left no doubt with numerous photographs posted in the articles that continued in the following days. In short, Japanese Judo was obscenely disparaged. It was a fine mess. Surprisingly there was one person who took the side of Japan and argued fervently in a newspaper article.

The author was an American man who had lived in the foreign settlement[29] in Nagasaki, Japan. He goes on to describe how he had collaborated with the Japanese man to publish a large book about Judo. Truly an impressive display of American ingenuity, to make the most of the situation and make a product for sale.[30]

---

[29] *Gaikokujin kyoryuchi* 外国人居留地 A foreign settlement was a special area in certain ports around Japan established to allow foreigners to live and work. There were seven of them in total. The system was begun in the mid 1858 and ended in 1899.

[30] This seems to be referring to John Joseph O'Brien (1865?-1930?) who also published his own version of a Jujutsu book.

COPYRIGHTED 1905 AMERICAN COLLEGE OF PHYSICAL CULTURE

PROF. JOHN J. O'BRIEN

who for ten years was Inspector of Police at Nagasaki, Japan, and who originally introduced Jiu-Jitsu into this country. Instructor of President Roosevelt, members of the Cabinet, and heads of departments in Washington, D.C.

At that time, Maeda also had a duel at Princeton University. It was with an American wrestler, and it was a very tough duel indeed. His opponent was naked.[31] So, he couldn't apply the more impressive Judo techniques. However, it was a great learning experience. So, this interesting episode will be detailed in the next chapter.

---

[31] *Ratai* 裸体 means "naked" but in this case meaning not wearing a Keikogi. Nowadays this would be simply "no-gi grappling" or "no gi wrestling."

第二勝 *Dainisho*
Second Victory

裸体角力 *Ratai Sumo*
Naked[32] Wrestling

In February, Maeda went to Princeton University to introduce Judo. At the time, there were several graduates from Waseda University studying abroad there, including Hattori, Yokoyama and three or four others. Maeda and company were taken immediately to the lecture and training hall. Once there they went to the changing room and put on their Keikogi. Mr. Hattori did the introductions and gave a brief overview of Japanese Judo and then Maeda and company moved to the center to demonstrate Judo Kata. Later, when they asked if anyone would like to train, they got three volunteers. The first was a gymnastics instructor at the school, another was a football champion at the school and the third was a wrestling champion.

That's when everything started to go sideways. Around this time wrestlers in America were beginning to think of Judo as a sort of for-profit scheme. Newspapers and magazines at the time were saying things like, "If Japanese Judoka don't wear a Keikogi, then they can't move well. Our eyes have been opened to their strange acrobatics and we won't be defeated by them anymore." In other words, peak "yellow journalism" was leveraged against us in the vulgar and fictious writings to drive out Japanese Judoka. As it turned out, some of the students at Princeton University had read such magazine and newspaper articles and now they challenged Maeda to a duel, albeit without a Keikogi.

"Well, if you don't want to wear a Keikogi, you all can feel free to train in your clothing!" Maeda retorted shortly. They insisted that training be done without a Keikogi. Maeda said, "Judo is different from Sumo, which is done with only a loincloth, in our country wresting shirtless is a different thing entirely. If you feel that it would be impossible to proceed unless we train without Keikogi,

---

[32] The author uses Ratai 裸体 meaning "naked" but this is referring to no-gi rather than wrestling completely nude.

then that is that. As for me, I have no desire to train without a Keikogi so we are done."

As it turned out, the Japanese students studying abroad leapt in and defended Maeda with the vociferousness that made it seem as if they were arguing over the return of Liaodong peninsula.[33] Indeed, they held their position and made their case in such a manner it would put the arguments of the high-ranking cabinet members to shame. This immediately put pressure on the conditions put forth by the Americans. They then turned to Maeda and said, "What if for some reason you were attacked by a person not wearing any clothing, what would a Judoka do in that situation."

This was a far-fetched scenario foisted as an argument by members of another school of martial arts. There is a difference between training and a real fight. There are many techniques that are not used during training and, if killing your attacker was not a concern, then being attacked by a naked assailant is not a problem. However, those techniques cannot be used during training. If it was a real fight, what kind of person would take hold of the attacker's collar with one hand and sleeve with the other, break his balance and then do some technique like Hiza-guruma? That is the stupidest thing Maeda had ever heard. Any person who even considered such a thing would get stomped to death in the process.

Today, Maeda and company had been invited to teach Judo, not engage in a duel. While they were not looking for a duel, if they did not duel these students into submission, then later Maeda and company would again be derided with accusations that Judo was not as effective as it claims to be. Even the Judo techniques they had carefully demonstrated risked being dismissed as theatrical acrobatics. If Maeda had been able to speak English fluently, he may have been able to explain kicks, strikes and the fundamental composition of Judo as well as the difference between Jissen, a real

---

[33] At the end of the Russo-Japanese War in 1905, both sides agreed to evacuate Manchuria and return it to China, with the exception of the Liaodong Peninsula which became part of Japan. After World War II, Liaodong became part of China again. As the treaty was not signed until September of 1905, they would not have been aware of the negotiations.

fight, and Keiko, training, however he had only been in America for less than a hundred days and that was simply beyond his capacity.

These men from a completely different system didn't seem to care about anything, they only wanted to see something different and unique, even if it was just to ridicule it. Thus, they now encouraged Maeda to forgo his Keikogi when dueling. The Americans were lined up in a rank and he was unable to dissuade them, putting him in a tough position. Though it was completely to his disadvantage, Maeda decided to agree to the duel without Keikogi.

However, while his first opponent, the football champion, took his shirt off, Maeda saw no reason to take off his Keikogi, so he left it on. The football champion was easily 6 Shaku, 180 cm, tall and had an impressive build. He was a youth that weight around 26 Kan, 98 kilograms. If you were set to fight in a life-or-death duel, one that is being framed as a practice-bout on the tatami mats, against a person who is half again as heavy as you, a head higher as well as being a champion sportsman, your prospects would not look good. Further, since this was in the era before Maeda became familiar with how these challenges worked, he ended up in a very difficult struggle indeed.

A famous person once said, "No matter how big a person may be, or how strong he is, there are no absolutes." That being said the speaker was referring to Judo being the most well-developed form of Taijutsu. [34] Philosophically speaking, if one person is knowledgeable in wrestling and the other is knowledgeable in Judo, the latter will have an advantage over the former. However, thinking a 5 Shaku, 150 cm, tall Judoka can handle a 6 Shaku, 180 cm, tall giant of a man both deftly and dramatically in the setting of training is to deny the reality of the situation. Against a turtle or a Japanese spaniel, a cat is quite superior. However, a cat's intensity and dexterity will hardly be enough for it to stand against a larger Japanese dog[35] or a lion.

---

[34] Taijutsu 体術 Any method of fighting that uses the body. Another word for Jujutsu.

[35] Nihoninu 日本犬 Literally "Japanese Dog" probably referring to a Shiba or Akita dog.

Maeda got lost in thought, considering how to handle this no-Keikogi bout with the Princeton University football player. If Maeda went to great effort and was able to throw him once or twice, that would be great training, however for a real duel he had to do the equivalent of completely stopping the breath in his opponent's body. Since this was not an actual fight, but a training exercise, dueling almost naked was a denial of the principal Maeda had previously explained. Training without a Keikogi meant that the duel was by the rules of Western wrestling. Judo had done a wonderful job advancing the arts of throwing, choking, and applying joint locks. However, if the opponent wasn't wearing any clothes, there was nothing to grab. This means that the duel becomes one like Western wrestling.

Since the only way to win was by pinning your opponent, a person using Western-style wrestling will be at an advantage. This is because they have spent long, painful hours learning how to suppress an opponent not wearing a Keikogi, far exceeding the training in that area done by Judoka. Moreover, in the real world, the chance that you will be facing an opponent wearing only a loincloth or completely nude is vanishingly small, so then training wrestling without any clothes on seems just like a playful diversion and not a form of self-defense.

Further, it would be a different matter if Maeda's opponent was a man of equivalent size, however since he was half again as large, it was bound to be a bone crushing fight. Trying to look at the problem objectively, Maeda realized that a large person wouldn't be able to move rapidly. So, if he paid attention, Maeda was unlikely to be thrown dramatically since his opponent would not be able to leap in quicky. On the defensive side, football player would be crouched down low like the Kana character く and rely on his long arms to grab hold of Maeda's arms. Maeda could sweep these away but then would be unable to use the refined leg techniques, hip throws and sacrifice throws developed by Judo.

This means that Maeda was in a tight spot if he wanted to win. The conditions of the match meant that Maeda was standing on death's door. He could try and shoot in deep or feint an opening to draw the football player in. By drawing his opponent in he could use that opening to apply his own technique. By charging into the opponent's breast pocket,[36] Maeda may be able to succeed with a good, clean throw. At any rate, he needed to break the football player's balance, force him to shift him from a defensive mode to a state where he is fearful. Maeda's only chance was to create that situation so he could employ his next gambit. This would mean entering close, like venturing into the tiger's lair, and his opponent was a giant, so there was a real danger of Maeda being crushed.

As it turned out the 6 Shaku tall man bent his body like the Kana character く and reached out expertly with arms that seemed longer than Maeda's whole body, successfully keeping him at bay. Maeda tried experimentally with Tsuri Dashi, a Sumo move where you hoist the opponent up by the belt, but the football player seemed prepared for this and brushed the attempt aside. He next tried Ashi Waza, leg techniques, but the football player maintained a wide stance with his legs bent at 90°angles like a town intersection, so these attacks proved ineffective. Koshi Nage, Seoi Nage, Seoi Otoshi, Maki-komi and other big throwing techniques were also clearly impossible to apply in this situation.[37]

---

[36] Futokoro ni Iru 懐に入る Refers to the place Japanese people would carry their valuables, inside the top of their Kimono. Also means "very close in."

[37] The author refers to Seoi Nage and Seoi Otoshi as Shoi Nage and Shoi Otoshi, which are alternate readings of the same Kanji.

Seoi Nage 1.   2.   3.   Seoi Otoshi

Illustrations from *An Instructor's Guide to Judo* 1936
By Yokoyama Sakujiro 横山作次郎(1869-1912)
  & Oshima Eisuke 大島英助(1865-1937)

Previously, Maeda had come up with a hundred different approaches and rejected them all before reevaluating them a second time. He had debated with himself to such a degree he had to chastise himself, "Do you think you have time to dwell on approaches given the situation?" With his mouth open he had stood rooted to the spot as his thoughts circled around and around inside his head, trying to work out his approach. His opponent would most likely be on the defense, working solely to prevent Maeda from approaching his sides. The fact that Maeda had forgotten to prepare a match and cigar in his front pocket was an error he would regret for the rest of his life.[38]

If his opponent was quick, he would be unlikely to give him a chance to ponder his next move. If his opponent rushed in quickly, the whole match would be easy. Alas, if he called a stop to the duel now, it would only result in mockery. Maeda could clearly see how refusing the duel would result in more scorn being heaped on Judo. It would be disparaged as being an art that is not as useful as it presumes to be. And despite the spectators witnessing the whole event, it would still be Maeda's responsibility. So, it seemed he had no choice but to enter the tiger's mouth.

Maeda shouted and leaped deep in towards the football player's center, setting up for Kata Guruma, Shoulder Wheel.[39] However, the

---

[38] This seems to be a joke along the lines of, "When pondering something, it's nice to have smoke."

[39] *Kata Guruma* 肩車 Shoulder Wheel from an early 20th century guide to Kodokan Judo.

opponent's body neither came unbalanced nor moved. As Maeda had lifted the football player's body up, his opponent had responded, whether by instinct or design, with the same thing that had happed the other day at officer training school West Point with Tomita Rokudan, namely the football champion wrapped up Maeda from behind. Maeda was now being handled like a ball. Was this going to be how it ended?

However, Maeda had learned something by watching Tomita Rokudan's match. Without panicking he put all his power in his arms and pushed as he drew his neck in, so that he wouldn't be smashed. Since his opponent was putting all his energy into this hold, Maeda responded by resisting with all his strength. As Maeda resisted, the football player didn't seem to have any more power to put into the hold, further it seemed as if his grip was slackening. Maeda rapidly freed his neck and, continuing that action tried to apply first Hikikomi-gaeshi, then Sumi-gaeshi...to no avail. Then Maeda planted his foot on the football players stomach before attacking with a technique that was an amalgam of Tomoe Nage and Hikikomi-gaeshi. [40] Maeda wasn't planning on doing any such technique, but this curious half-and-half technique is what naturally came to him during this duel. Hikikomi-gaeshi and Sumi-gaeshi are two techniques that only very rarely appear on the mats in the

---

[40] *Hikikomi-gaeshi, Sumi-gaeshi* and *Tomoe Nage* from an early 20th century guide to Kodokan Judo.
Hikikomi-gaeshi 引込返 ・ *Sumi-gaeshi* 隅返 ・ *Tomoe Nage* 巴投

Kodokan, however these techniques are a testament to the meticulous vision of Kano Shihan, who began this school. In a duel against a different school these techniques can be applied quite naturally.

Since Maeda's technique was applied from an unexpected angle, it was a success and the giant football player flew through the air, tracing a half-circle over Maeda's head before crashing to the ground. Maeda needed to wrap his opponent up before he rose from the ground or else he would no doubt escape and guard against Maeda's approach. Thus, having finished throwing his opponent across the room, Maeda rolled quickly to his feet. Unfortunately, he found his opponent was also as nimble as a monkey and had recovered about the same time as Maeda. Be that as it may, the giant man was still a bit dazed from having been thrown in a dramatic fashion and his body appeared to not be totally under his control as he stood somewhat awkwardly. "This is it" thought Maeda and he wrapped the man up from behind and set up for an Ura Nage. The giant football player responded by bending his body into the shape of the Kana character く almost the point where he was crawling on the ground.

Realizing his original attack would not work, Maeda shifted to Yoko-guruma. That too did not take, and though Maeda's positioning was poor he did not want to give the man any reprieve, so he wrapped up the enemy's waist from behind and hauled down. Since he had pursued his opponent this far and maintained pressure by applying one technique after another, it would have been wasted effort to simply let go of him. Holding his opponent's hips to the ground meant he couldn't escape, and Maeda decided he very much would like to slam him to the ground with an Ura Nage, reverse throw, that would shake the ground with a powerful Ippon.[41]

---

[41] Ura Nage 裏投 "Reverse Throw" from an early 20th century guide to Kodokan Judo.

Typically when an opponent's hips are held low, he will at some point seek to rise up. Maeda pressed his opponent's hips forward from behind, expecting him to resist in the opposite direction. However, this man used the pressure Maeda was applying from behind to assist him as he shot forward, diving off the mats, dragging Maeda behind him. Such appalling bald-faced cowardice made a shameful mockery of American grit. When it looked like he was going to lose he exited the training circle, thereby escaping a dangerous situation. This was how a university student was behaving!

The people watching announced, "You are off the mats! Move back in! Move back in!" Thus all Maeda's efforts to stay locked to his opponent's hips were blown away like foam bubbles. Maeda pulled his opponent back onto the mats by his waist, so the football player returned to the ring with Maeda still holding on to him. However, he still had one foot outside the mats. Since the agreement was a match cannot be decided outside the mats, Maeda's opponent chose this cowardly way. When Maeda had seen a chance to throw,

his opponent had managed to get both feet off the mats and, having succeeded in doing that, the relief was plain on the football player's face. Maeda was once again put in a tough spot.

Next, as the way of the warrior meant dealing the hand you were dealt, Maeda intentionally pushed his opponent towards the edge of the mats. This caused his opponent to resist by putting power in the leg towards the edge of the mats. Maeda then pulled him towards the center of the mats, causing his opponent to put power in the opposite leg, pushing toward the area outside the mats. Maeda rotated his body to the outside and shoved his opponent strongly towards the center. The football player refused to budge and dropped his body into a shape like the Kana く and immediately resisted. "I've got him!" Maeda thought as he used this opportunity apply an explosive Ura Nage. He had set the throw up perfectly and the opponent's body traced a beautiful half circle before dropping outside the mats. The man slammed his back into the floorboards with a terrific crash, and clearly in a great deal of pain, signaled his defeat.

If his opponent had been wearing a Keikogi, the affair would have been wrapped up in short order. However, since Maeda's opponent had been shirtless it took a spectacularly long time and required no small effort. When written down, the duel seems quite long. However, from start to finish, only around ten minutes had elapsed. However, due to the physical and mental toil the duel seemed to have taken much longer. The fact that the fake Judoka and the American from the other day had spent an hour and a half holding onto each other's collar seems as silly as a man pondering a single thought for a hundred years.

第三勝 *Daisansho*
Third Victory

Shukyu no Senshu
Soccer Champion

Following the 6 Shaku football champion the next challenger was a gymnastics teacher at Princeton University. He was slightly taller than Maeda but seemed to weigh about the same. "This looks like an even match." Maeda thought. Looking his opponent over, Maeda figured he would be quick and nimble. He was not wearing a Keikogi and had a haughty look about him that seemed to say, "I should be able to beat this guy without any undo effort."

Both combatants shook hands and the gymnastics teacher dropped back several steps and dropped his hips. His stance reminded Maeda of a cat stalking a rat. If compared to a Japanese Sumo wrestler, it would be like how Tamatsubaki[42] crouched low. In this situation Maeda wasn't going to let his opponent dictate how the match would flow. He wasn't going to grunt *Un!* and drop into a low, tense stance as that would be to his disadvantage. That was appropriate for Sumo wrestling. However, it wasn't how Judo was done. A Judoka is going to make use of the opponent's power; thus it was better for Maeda to keep his opponent's entire body in view while his own body stood naturally, waiting for his opponent to jump in. At this point Maeda was focusing all his power on breathing while his opponent was just wasting his strength.

Maeda seemed to be standing carelessly, however he was hardly careless as he was watching every part of his opponent's body. He could clearly see his opponent thinking that Maeda must be weakened from his previous bout. While the gymnastics teacher was tensed and ready, his Judoka opponent was just sort of drifting, without any tension. Surely the gymnast was thinking, "He must not be ready and while he is not focused this is the best moment to leap in!"

---

[42] Referring to the Sumo wrestler Tamatsubaki Kentaro 玉椿憲太郎 (1883 ~1928,) who was active at the time. Though he was only 158 cm tall and weighed 73 kg, he handled larger opponents deftly.

Just as Maeda anticipated, his opponent darted in like a flying bird. Maeda wrapped up his attacker's left arm and dropped down doing a side sacrifice-throw called Uki-waza.[43] Since his timing had been so perfect not even a gap large enough for a hair to slide through existed, the opponent was thrown and struck his head and shoulder hard as he rolled. However, in a measure of the man's bravery, the gymnast had nimbly gotten to his feet and before Maeda had completely risen, he leapt, trying to pin Maeda. The crowd of students was cheering wildly from all sides, mistakenly thinking that because the Judoka was being pinned, he was in danger of losing. Maeda soon flipped his opponent over, so he was on top. The gymnast was roughly the same weight as Maeda, so it was not much of a challenge. Further, if he had been wearing a Keikogi, Maeda could have handled him as he liked, even going so far as to demonstrate a visually impressive Kata by throwing him with a big technique. However, since his opponent was shirtless, Maeda had to be cautions, and any sort of flashy display of his skill would have to wait for another time.

Having flipped his opponent over, Maeda locked him with Kesa Gatame. His opponent was struggling mightily to avoid having both shoulders touch the mats. For Maeda, it didn't matter whether both shoulders were touching the mats or not. Eventually a strangled cry of "I give" echoed up from below him.

Maeda released the man and stood up. For his next attack,

---

[43] *Uki Waza* 浮業 "floating throw" from an early 20th century guide to Kodokan Judo.

Maeda grabbed him from behind and threw with an Ura Nage hard enough so it seemed it would bury him in the mats. He followed by applying a Gyaku, joint lock, to his bent arm, causing him to yield.

This gymnastics instructor, in contrast to the football player, while light on his feet and nimble of movement was strangely easier to handle.

The third challenger declined his chance to duel. Whether that was dude to fear or lack of time was unclear, at any rate the session had ended without any trouble. As far as an "introduction to Judo" Maeda was not very satisfied with how things had gone. On one hand, he had been able to bounce his opponent along the floor with a throw in the previous technique, but, during training he would have been able to execute a much cleaner throw. He satisfied himself with the thought that at least the newspaper reporters would not be able to lie about the outcome of today's duel. Maeda regretted he had not been able to show what he was unable to describe in words, mainly to make the practitioners of other sports realize what kind of beautiful techniques are possible in Judo

A few days later, Maeda was notified that about 20 students from Princeton expressed interest in Judo and would he be interested in teaching a class? So, he went and taught twice a week at Princeton University.

A JUDO WARRIOR'S JOURNEY AROUND THE GLOBE・世界横行柔道武者修業

道場開き *Dojo Biraki*
Opening a Dojo

Around this time, the American, who had previously lived in Nagasaki, had published a large book on Judo. He had worked with a fake-Judoka, using him as a product, to complete the volume. While the cover of the book proclaims it to be "Kano Judo," it is filled with many incomprehensible pictures of wrists being twisted and legs being bent. The descriptions aren't even articulate enough to fool a child. In short, the book had little value. However, since American's love new and rare things. they were virtually in a competition to shove forward five dollars to snatch up a copy.[44]

---

[44] The book Maeda refers to is, "The Complete Kano Jiu-jitsu" by Hancock and Katsumata, first published in 1905.

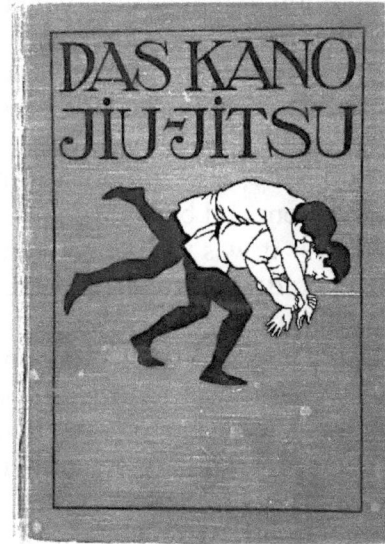 

Right: Harrie Hancock (1868 ~ 1922) A prolific writer of young adult fiction, including a fictional depiction of a German invasion of the United States. Hancock worked in the Philippines as a reporter and thus, may also have been in Nagasaki at some point.
Left: Higashi Katsumata 東勝熊 (1881~?) A Jujutsu practitioner active in America and Europe. He began studying Jujutsu at the age of 9. He may have studied Shiten Ryu 四天流 Jujutsu.

So why then don't American publishers work with a real Judoka on producing a book? That is because true Judoka prioritize their responsibility and will not agree to allow a half-assed book to be published. We would demand every aspect be considered and will not allow anything less than a perfect representation, which would cost time and money. This is something that is anathema to the American way of doing business, which seeks to tabulate everything in a record book kept in the breast pocket.

This carried over to the classes Maeda ran at the YMCA. Initially, there were 10 students. But after two months, less than half were still training. At Princeton University, while the students had initially been passionate about training, their fervor gradually waned. The first program was set to run for 6 weeks. Once that finished, a second six-week program was proposed, however only one-third of the students were interested. This, coupled with the two-hour round trip train journey from New York, in addition to purchasing dinner, meant that the salary was no longer sufficient.

Around this time, they met a man in New York who was operating an exercise space and wondered if they might be interested in opening a Dojo in the same space. Since Maeda and Tomita wanted to teach their school in New York City, why not open it in his space? They quickly came to an agreement and began using the space. It was not particularly large however it was well appointed. After training, they could use either hot or cold water freely to bathe. It was perfect for their training and teaching needs.

So, now that Maeda had opened his Dojo, he had a problem. How was he to use this Dojo to spread his name as a well-qualified Judo Sensei widely amongst the people? The owner of the Dojo recommended running advertisements, since if nobody came then no matter how great the Dojo or how great the Sensei, it can't function. Thus, they started out by running advertisements which resulted in one or two prospective students. Meanwhile Maeda continued with the lessons at Princeton University and he and Tomita taught at the YMCA. If they didn't have classes, then they worked at the Dojo. At the same time, they were going around to all the YMCA locations, gyms, and other sports organizations and conducting demonstrations. However, the result was much like before, they would show a Kata, and ask, "So then, would anyone like to try Judo?" and no one would volunteer. Invariably there would be 2 or 3 rather large fellows that would step forward smug in their abilities. However, as they lacked stability in their hips, they got thrown in dramatic fashion, before being finished off with a Gyaku, joint lock, which caused them to surrender. Maeda and Tomita proceeded in this fashion for a while.

As for the Dojo, they would get a new student or two nearly every day, however most would not continue for long. Just when they were thinking that the number of students was increasing, a student who had been training regularly would stop attending. It seemed the number of students hovered just about 10. No matter how you looked at it, this was not enough to run a Dojo. The character of Americans meant that they are passionate about new things, however if after 10 or 20 days you don't act like they are on the verge of becoming a great judo practitioner or you throw them a bit harder than usual, then they don't show up the next day.

Maeda decided, "We must run one dramatic challenge in the paper, inviting an American wrester or boxing champion to a public bout. That way the people can finally see with their own eyes that there is a true Judo Sensei." This was the beginning of Maeda's life of public duels.

So, Maeda began on his plan to publicly announce himself by name, offering challenges to people. In New York you could find many kinds of Dojo. There were wrestling, sword fighting, boxing, and other kinds of schools that were all bustling with students. However, all the Sensei at these Dojo had first made their name by offering open challenges in order to gain recognition. They had then used that fame to attract students and therefore succeed when they opened their Dojo. At this time, even men such as the legendary military strategists Zhuge Liang (181~234 AD) and Jiang Ziya (1200 ~1100 BC,) would have been setting up shop here as they would not have found an audience in their homeland of China. In short, everyone in the world was gathering in America and setting up in a cheap apartment and saying, "I am a Judo Sensei and Champion!" In the face of this bragging, the people living nearby no doubt lambasted their disagreeable east Asian neighbors.

When Maeda proposed his plan to hold a duel at the Dojo, the owner was overjoyed. "I know a newspaper reporter, so I will have a talk with him!" he announced, throwing himself into the project with enthusiasm. The owner understood that if the Dojo did well, then his profits would increase, so this passion originated from considering his pocketbook. He quickly contacted his friend at the newspaper and three days later a reporter came and observed Maeda's lesson, and soon the agreement for the duel was signed, which got everyone swinging into motion.

In America. a contract for these kinds of duels can only be finalized by an intermediary. Professional fighters will hold a match at a public arena and charge an admission fee or both sides will place a bet. Even if a professional fighter loses the bout, he still gets some of the money, otherwise there wouldn't be a wouldn't fight. The only people that set up bouts for fun are students or amateurs. In such a fight, even if you win, you won't receive any acclaim.

Setting up a bout at a public arena and charging admission is basically a fight for entertainment. However, having a duel in front of the public serves to introduce yourself to the entirety of society. It is not being done to create a spectacle. An argument can be made that since Maeda was the one who originated the event, which is being merchandised, he is "selling a spectacle" however the sales aspect of the event is being completely handled by a merchant and Maeda's role is solely to be the one stepping out onto the stage and dueling his opponent. Since Maeda will only be paid for his effort, this was the way he set it up.

If there are still some that think this is an unacceptable way to do things, then the Waseda University baseball team is just as guilty, as are any writers or researchers who accept money for publishing articles in magazines. Those that give speeches about how they are doing everything they can for the country, meaning everything to ensure they continue as a cabinet minister, who enjoy lavish lifestyles are also out of line. The only good ones are the peasants that pick up their hoe every day and work in the fields. By this logic all 50 million Japanese should just spend their day working on their own farm.

Maeda had become friendly with the reporter and eagerly awaited news on who his opponent would be. The reporter, for his part, seemed to believe in Maeda's ability and therefore worked diligently at the project. However, as time passed, he received no word from the reporter. One day, after becoming tired of waiting, Maeda went to the owner of the Dojo and asked him what was going on. The owner, looking dejected, answered with a question, "Weren't you the one to cancel the bout?"

This curious question made Maeda feel like he was in a dream. The owner continued, "The fact is, that newspaper reporter was doing his best to find an opponent for you and was talking with people all over town. Word of his search reached the ears of some Japanese living in New York, and they thought it sounded suspicious. A Japanese man confronted the reporter and told him that under no circumstances would a Kodokan Judoka, a man who believes in Yamato-damashi[45] and the flowering of Bushido, would ever agree to duel with someone as low-character as an American wrestler from the bowels of society. Kano Sensei has spoken specifically against this sort of thing. The Japanese man was convinced the reporter had conspired with me, the owner of Dojo, and that we were using Maeda as a pawn in order to drink the sweet soup of profit from this entertainment. He said, "Your suspicious plot has been exposed and now this duel should be immediately cancelled." I presumed that you had met with that man and decided to call off the whole thing?"

Maeda stood there as if he had been struck by a bolt of lightning out of a clear sky.

---

[45] Yamatao-damashi 大和魂 The Japanese spirit.

第四勝 *Daiyonsho*
Fourth Victory

Koronbia Daigaku wo Shime-otosu
Choking Out a Student at Columbia University

A large part of a Samurai's life was not spent in literary pursuits but wild violence. At any moment Samurai might be sent forward into battle, to die before their lord. That is what they were made for, nothing else. Thus Bushido, the way of the warrior, the path that Samurai followed in the Edo period is not applicable in the twentieth century, it does not make any sense for it to apply in America.

Is an American wrestler even lower in status than a Sumo wrestler in Ryogoku? [46] How about if the Sumo wrestler Tamatsubaki dripped sweat on the Tatami mats at the Kodokan? If the discussion were about confirming American wrestlers as our

---

[46] Ryogoku 両国 is a part of Tokyo that has long had many Sumo stables (training halls.) A designated Sumo hall began to be used in 1909. Before that tournaments were held on the grounds of shrines or temples. The matches were called *Kanjin-zumo* 勧進相撲, or benefit sumo for shrines and temples, in order to collect donations for the upkeep of the religious buildings.

"The matches proved immensely popular, but reached the stage where all money was going towards the wages of the "Sumotori", rather than the original cause. In this case too, there were also many cases of brawling, especially when people were called up from the crowd to participate."

-Nicole Bargwanna *A SERIOUS SIDE TO SUMO* 1996

Since there were only two tournaments a year, each lasting 10 days there was a saying that went:

Sumo is an occupation that requires only twenty days of annual work

"The reality, however, was not so easy as it seems as the wrestlers had to go on local exhibition tours and do other odd jobs for their sponsoring domain in addition to the twenty days of the regular tournaments."

-Tokyo Metropolitan Library Exhibit

stepbrothers through ceremonial Sake drinking, that would be a problem. However, comparing the techniques used by American wrestlers with Japanese Judo is not really a matter of low class or high class. At this point Maeda and company were in far off New York, so the thinking and wisdom of the Samurai of Japan was clearly not applicable in this situation, and it only serves to bedevil the Judoka. Since Americans seem to be fearful of Judo as if it is magic, maybe they feel there is a little of the devil's handiwork in Judo.

Maeda set to work thinking on the problem and he decided that he had to proceed with his plan to duel with members of the American wrestling association. It was fate. He told the owner of the Dojo about his decision. "Someone I don't even know got involved in the situation and now we must start over from the beginning. For now, however I will remain quiet and wait for the next chance for a duel."

Around this time Maeda finally got a response to their first offer, the one they made to the University of Colombia when they first arrived. He received a letter asking him to give a demonstration and lecture one evening. So, Maeda and Tomita practiced the techniques they were going to teach, and the next morning set out for the University.

The order they taught was first Nage Kata, then Koshiki Kata, Taiso Kata and finally Shobu Kata. From there Maeda did practice-Randori with the strongest looking student of the bunch. For his part, the student intended to make it a duel and put all his effort into defeating Maeda. However, since today everyone was wearing a Keikogi and, by this point, Maeda had become familiar with dueling with other schools of martial arts, it was quite easy. There were also wives and socialites in attendance, so no one seemed inclined to request to take their Keikogi off. In fact, there were people wearing socks. Thus, Maeda could throw, sweep or show Kata as he pleased. Throughout the event, interest in the proceedings showed on the faces of the students.

Finally, Maeda did a collar choke on the student and after a moment he dropped to the ground. The scene turned into one of pandemonium as the women observing in the crowd shrieked and all the faces of the students went pale. "There is nothing to worry about!" Maeda said in a calm voice as he administered Katsu, resuscitation, causing the lad to resume breathing normally. The crowd was stunned.

Next Tomita Rokudan armed himself with a Tessen, iron fan, and Maeda took up a Katana. They proceeded to demonstrate four or five rather dramatic techniques with the two weapons. The audience was fascinated by this display and their hearts were clearly moved. There was a loud applause that didn't seem like it was ever going to end. As it turned out the demonstration did not focus as heavily on Kata, but this kind of energetic and varied demonstration of techniques seemed to be well-suited to the curious nature of a foreign audience.

Maeda and Tomita had finally made headway at Columbia University which was the first place they had approached about teaching Judo after arriving in New York. Following the demonstration, they got a letter from the school stating that there were five or six students looking to train. Since five or six people wasn't enough to make a class, they wrote back requesting at least ten people, but they never heard back. Columbia University, unlike Yale, Harvard and Princeton, did not have the same passion for sports. The students' clothes were very refined and gentlemanly.

第五勝 *Daigosho*
Fifth Victory

New York Taiiku Kurubu
New York Athletic Club

So, in the end, the first place they tried, Columbia University did not turn out in their favor. Basically, they were working at three places: a few students at the YMCA, Princeton University and the Dojo. Next, they received an invitation to do a demonstration and lecture at the New York Athletic Club. This was around the middle of March in Meiji 38, 1905. When they arrived at the prescribed date, they found that club seemed to be full of very wealthy members. The club itself was in a fine building and the facility was very well appointed.

They proceeded with the demonstration as before, and after showing Kata, Maeda ended up paired with the club champion for training. It seemed no matter where he went someone wanted to test Maeda's ability and limits. Thought Maeda had gone to the demonstration expecting this, Tomita would not do such training, only Maeda.

This champion was a heavy wrestler, weighing 250 Kin, which is 30 Kan or 113 kilograms. However, since neither Maeda nor Tomita spoke the language, they usually relied on someone who spoke English to explain. The original plan was of course to train, however that had shifted to a duel. Maeda wanted to confirm a few conditions before the bout to avoid difficulties later. As it turned out the man translating was not doing a very good job. Since the man was doing Maeda a favor and was clearly trying his best to explain that in Judo, the shoulders touching the mats isn't a problem, and that if chokes or joint locks begin to become unbearable to signal by tapping. However, the translator was unable to convey this basic bit of understanding between competitors before starting. The translator didn't have an understanding of Judo, so the other side was misunderstanding. He was a nice person and trying to help, so Maeda felt it he shouldn't interfere, so he asked a salesman to try and confirm everything and that turned out to be a good decision.

Eventually the duel between Maeda and the giant 30 Kan

wrestler began. He was tall and looked very strong and if the man stayed on the defensive, this would be a very tough match indeed. The bout began and Maeda immediately grabbed both of his sleeves and was thinking "Should I pull him or push him?" when he sensed that the giant man was not particularly skilled. Maeda first thought to apply a Koshi Waza, hip throw, but being cautious he pushed a little first, then tested him out by lifting his arms up. Since his opponent was wholly unfamiliar with Judo, he immediately resisted by pushing forward with all his power. Seeing that this man was an easy target, Maeda planted his right foot on the man's abdomen and kicked him over in a Tomoe Nage, causing him to trace a huge arc in the air.

This infuriated the man who had allowed a small Jap to defeat him, and his face flushed red as he charged in again full power.[47] Maeda immediately applied Tsurikomi-goshi and made the room shake with the power of his throw. When the man rose, Maeda threw him again with Tai-otoshi.[48] Considering the man weighed 30 Kan, Maeda was probably overdoing it, however he set the technique up

---

[47] "Jap" is written as Jyappu ヂャップ with Nihonjin "Japanese" 日本人 written over it in Kanji.

[48] Illustrations from *An Easy Illustrated Guide to Judo* 通俗柔道図解 by Arima Sumitomo 1905.

    Tai Otoshi 体落 "Body Drop"   Tsurikomi Goshi 釣込腰
                                              "Lifting and Pulling Hip Throw"

perfectly and the man traced a huge wheel in the air before slamming to the ground. A beautiful Waza. As it turned out however, the man showed no signs of slackening his attacks, no matter how many times Maeda threw him, he kept getting back up and attacking relentlessly in the same reckless manner. Finally, after throwing him a final time, Maeda applied the choke Okuri Eri-jime and with a gurgling sound, the man dropped.[49]

So, as you might expect it was a drama, three of the club's managers as well as two or three other people rushed forward, their faces gone pale, telling Maeda to stop. Maeda released his grip, and the crowd was startled to see the man's face turned from a bright pink to a dark red. The giant man had been utterly defeated and withdrew. After that, Maeda was able to train for a few minutes with a Japanese man who knew a little bit about Judo. All in the demonstration went very well.

As it turns out the next day when he looked at the paper, Maeda and Tomita were again slandered through use of the Yellow Journalism style of writing. Line after line spoke ill of Maeda and company, dismissing the match with the words, "In yesterday's bout, the American who agreed to duel wearing a Keikogi, had the unfortunate luck to be thrown two or three times." Nowhere did the article mention that while Maeda weighed 18 Kan, 68 kilograms, the American weighted close to 30 Kan, 113 kilograms. Finally, with

---

[49] *Okuri Eri Jime* 送襟絞 "Sliding collar strangle" from *How to Become Expert at Judo* 柔道上達法 1939.

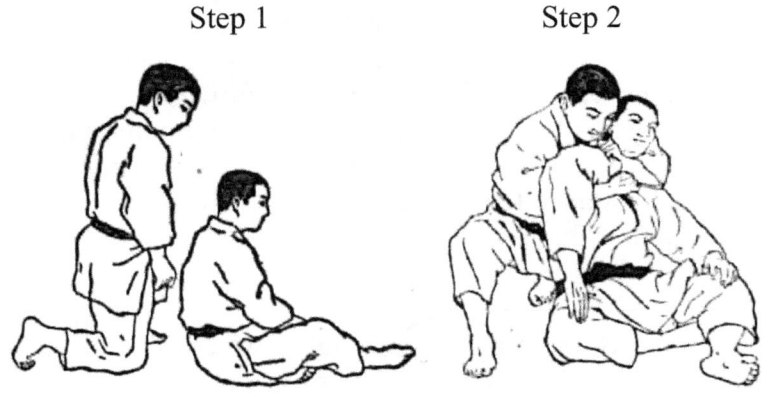

Step 1   Step 2

regards to the American dropping from being choked, the article implied the exact opposite occurred, that Maeda was unable to rise.

Maeda and company shook their heads with a dry laugh, "What are the American newspapers talking about?" Such an article demanded they protest vociferously and demand a full retraction. It seemed clear the giant man, to rehabilitate his image, had bribed the reporter. If you are talking of low-class or inferiority, these professional wrestlers are even worse than student wrestlers. The other day when Maeda dueled at Princeton University, his opponent was an officer and according to the paper Maeda had only won due to cowardly tactics. Could this be America-damashi?[50]

As it turns out another newspaper wrote the following, "Yesterday at the New York Athletic Club, the champion Deek Bough got treated like a child's ball by the Japanese Judoka Maeda. His face got red as fire!" Reading this helped relieve Maeda's heartburn.

Around this time the snow began to melt, and the Japanese men could feel the heat of the sun on their skin. Since spring was beginning the season of indoor training was almost at an end. On April 1st they responded to an invitation from the Chicago City Athletic Club for a lecture and demonstration. It was a twenty-hour train ride from New York. When they arrived, there was a tournament at the club and many kinds of athletic events were occurring. It was like the sports festivals at Japanese schools.

Outside the sports stadium there were a lot of barriers and entrance points for spectators to pay admission. Since everything was so strict outside, they went back in. They did their demonstration inside the stadium. The whole facility was very wide and well appointed, surprising Maeda and company. The facility could easily accommodate tens of thousands of spectators, who would watch the various athletes compete in different contests. The sports festival was set to start in the evening and last until midnight every day for the next three days, so people didn't have to take time off work. The entrance fee was used to offset the cost of the event and the remaining money went to supporting the club. From the

---

[50] The author is asking if this is the "soul of America" much like "Yamato-damashi" describes the "soul of Japan."

perspective of Bushido, this would probably look suspiciously like entertainment, however Maeda was unable to find an American that spoke out against it and the club was able to continue its activates since it was well off. It seemed this method was extremely good at allowing them to continue to run their organization. Since Maeda and company were only contracted for one night, they were able to see a great number of American-style athletic competitions. The next day, having finished their Judo demonstration they walked around Chicago, looking at the sights. The day after that they boarded a train for New York.

At this point perhaps an explanation of how Japanese Judoka were dispersed around America would be interesting.

紐育の梁山泊 *New York no Ryozanpaku*
The New York Assemblage of the Bold and Ambitious

When Maeda and company sailed for America, the elder statesman of the Kodokan Yamashita Nanadan[51] was in Washington DC, spending all his time teaching Judo. Yamashita Nanadan had arrived in America a year earlier at the invite of the man known as "King of the Railroad" Samuel Hill.[52] The reason for the invite was so Hill's children could learn Judo. However, his wife, Mrs. Hill, was against the plan. So, Hill arranged for his alma mater Harvard University to create a Judo class and soon several dozen students were taking lessons from Yamashita Nanadan. Later, he began teaching at the Naval Academy as well. The period when he was in Washington DC teaching President Teddy Roosevelt was just prior to this.

When Maeda and company were in New York, due to our victories in the Russo-Japanese War, there was a great deal of positive feeling toward Japan, and their Judo lectures and demonstrations had a positive influence as well. Now, no matter where they went, they were greeted with extremely positive praise along the lines of, "Japanese Judo is a secret technique. It is certainly of divine creation, as it is a method of barehanded fighting with no equal in the world. How else could 5 Shaku, 150-centimeter, Japanese soldiers defeat 6 Shaku, 180-centimeter, Russian soldiers. It is because they study Judo."

At this point starting a Japanese Judo Society would have been a good move, and it wasn't like they were several different political parties, so proceeding with such a plan would have been profitable and many were open to the prospect. If the Judoka in Washington and New York joined up they could try to expand their activities together. However, it did not work out in the end.

At any rate, the season for training outside had begun and Maeda's contracts at Princeton University and the YMCA were coming to an end, so he was only training with the few members of

---

[51] *Nanadan* 七段 Seventh degree black belt.
[52] Samuel Hill (1857 ~1931) was a railroad executive and businessman.

his New York Dojo.

In May, members of the Waseda University baseball team came to America to play. Accompanying the baseball team was Ono Sandan, who sent Maeda a message from Washington DC. [53]

Ono Sandan was staying in DC and acting as an assistant to Yamashita Nanadan. In his remaining time Ono was teaching at the Naval Academy in Annapolis. Kawaguchi Shodan was also serving as a temporary assistant to Yamashita Nanadan in Washington, however he soon came to New York and stayed with Maeda and company. In addition, Kyono Nidan also arrived and with Tomita Rokudan as the head, the five of them made a fine group. They were in such high spirits neither arrows nor rifles could dissuade their revelry[54].

Unfortunately, the season was the season and hot days followed.

---

[53] "An exemplar of Kodokan Judo, Ono Akitaro 大野秋太郎 in April of 1908."

[54] A variation of the expression *Ya demo Teppo demo Mottekoi* 矢でも 鉄砲でも持って来い "Come with arrows or come with Rifles!" An expression which invites an opponent to attack in any way he sees fit.

Training inside became impossible and the Dojo went on hiatus. The five of them went frequently to the Dojo however it didn't work out because they couldn't muster the enthusiasm. They had come halfway around the earth and training only with each other had them at a loss. Since none of the five could speak the language, they passed their time in their rooms doing nothing in particular. At the Kodokan all these men strutted around as part of the "bigger Judoka." However, in America, though there were a great number of patrolmen larger than the Sumo wrestler Hitachiyama[55] on patrol and keeping law and order, the five men were very small. Whenever they walked around town they were mistaken for Chinese men or even children, judging by the talking behind their backs they heard.

Maeda wrote a challenge and sent it to the newspaper; however he never got any response and the five men continued to pass the time not doing anything in particular, which caused them to fret about their forced idleness. One man got irritated and said, "We should find a bar and get some wine or something." Another said, "I want nothing more than to have a meal of this years hulled rice and miso soup." Another man's solution was, "Maybe I will dress up as a stable-hand and start a fight and see how far I can throw some giant man."

---

[55] Referring to the Sumo Wrestler Hitachiyama Taniemon 常陸山 (1874~1922) From 1903 ~ 1914 he was Yokozuna ranked. He was very large, 1.74 meters tall and weighed 146 kilograms.

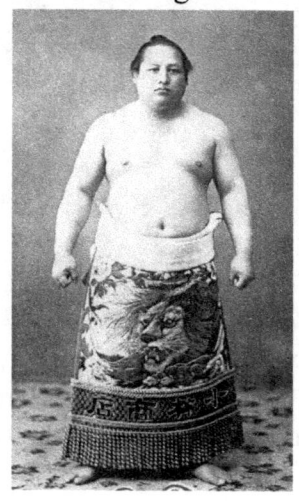

All of them desired to test their muscles and push their limits. Maeda recalled the planned duel that had been cancelled due to someone's interference and regretted all that effort had been washed away.

So, though the Japanese martial artists had formed "an assemblage of the bold and ambitious" in one corner of New York, they were quite discouraged. The group supported one another and eventually decided to make a big move. They would find a way to announce themselves as Tenka-Muteki, warriors undefeated and without equal under the heavens.

第六勝 *Dairokusho*
Sixth Victory

Tenka Wakeme no Kokaisen
Public Duel to Find the True Champion

So, these five Kodokan men had established themselves in one corner of New York City. They were in a funk and rolled about their rooms not doing much of anything like the Chinese General Liu Bei (161 ~ 223) who returned to his straw hut no fewer than three times. But time and tide wait for no man, and they realized there was not enough money to pay their lodging fees. Thus, each man struck out on his own.

First of all, Maeda found work in an area a few miles from New York City, the famous summer getaway spot near Coney Island called Manhattan Beach. There was a Japanese community there and he was hired to teach Judo twice a week. So he and the Japanese that lived there trained Kata and Randori. Maeda even took the step of erecting a sign saying, "If anyone would like to challenge me, I will gladly accept!" This Manhattan Beach was a famous place for people to summer, and with so many people in the same place Maeda felt he was bound to get someone to take him up on his offer.

On the other hand, Ono Sandan linked up with some Japanese students studying at Yale University and set off to introduce Judo in Ashville, North Carolina in America's southern area. Tomita Rokudan went to the beach of Newport, Rhode Island and found some students at that summer retreat.

It was around this time that the news of the complete obliteration of the Russian Baltic Fleet arrived in the form of a special edition newspaper, which excited all of America. This was June 27th of Meiji 38, 1905, which was actually the day before it was announced in Japan.

Just as June shifted to July, an American wrestler responded to Maeda's public challenge. He was known in the American wrestling world as "Butcher Boy" and was reported to be very strong. He sent a photograph of himself along with his response to the challenge. They agreed on the rules for the duel.

1. Both parties shall wear a Japanese-style Keikogi.
2. The fighters will only use Gyaku, Shime and Nage. However, throws will only count if both shoulders touch the ground. The same applies for Oshikomi, pins. Gyaku and Shime, or joint locks and chokes, will not count until the opponent signals his defeat.[56] With those points agreed upon, both sides agreed on a date and signed the agreement.

At last, the day of the duel arrived. The place was the Japanese village on Manhattan Beach, and since it was the end of July at the

---

[56] John Piening "Butcher Boy" (1876 ~ ?)

Two excellent portraits of John Piening, showing wonderful development of neck, chest and arms.

summer retreat there were a great many spectators. There were even many Japanese from around Washington DC and New York, so that the crowd ended up more than half Japanese. Was this due to Maeda having travelled numerous times to various Universities and dueled with local wrestlers? Those were not public exhibitions, so most Japanese living in the States were not aware of Maeda's ability. Further, even though he had defeated strong opponents at universities and other places, the newspapers had lied about the incident, slandering Maeda and company. No doubt there were many Hanshin-Hangi, half-believing, half-not-believing Japanese in attendance. Another attendee was the fake "Great Judo Sensei" from the other day. His ill-advised deal with his American partner had led to him being defeated in an embarrassing way. Now he came to watch the duel, worried about what would happen.

Amongst the Japanese there were some who, judging by the color of their faces, were very concerned. Some of them flat out recommended violence in excited tones, "You cannot be defeated this time! Do whatever you have to but don't let that guy beat you, even if you have to choke him to death or break his arm!" For his part Maeda was committed to winning this bout. His compatriots were also rooting for him to win. If he lost this bout, it would completely overshadow the humiliating loss by the arrogant self-proclaimed Great Judo Sensei to the American wrestler. If he lost today, the chance to expand Judo in America would also be lost. Maeda felt that this was a test of fate to decide if he was a true champion. He felt this in his entire body and his muscles began to twitch of their own volition in anticipation.

The time to start the match arrived and both parties proceeded to the center of the ring. The referee and the timekeeper conferred, and Maeda and the American wrestler shook hands before stepping back and glaring at one another. As it turns out Butcher Boy was a fairly famous name in wrestling. He was almost 6 Shaku[57], 180 centimeters, tall and nearly 30 Kan, 113 kilograms. His body was well developed and he was covered with muscles that moved under his skin. In short, he looked very strong, though he seemed to be not

---

[57] I'm beginning to get the impression that 6 Shaku just means "really tall" and 30 Kan is another word for "really heavy."

used to wearing a Keikogi and it looked a bit strange on him. His eyes were deep-set into his head but glittered with a fierce light at 5 Shaku 4 Sun, 162 cm, Maeda. To Maeda it seemed like the man looked down on him scornfully, as if saying, "Look at this tiny Jap! I will crush him with one squeeze of my hand." With that he extended his long arms and charged in recklessly. This kind of opponent, who just rushes in headlong, is exactly what Judoka hope for. The moment he closed in to make contact, Maeda rotated his body to the left, snatched both his sleeves and applied Tai Otoshi. Typically, Tai Otoshi is an extremely bad choice against a larger opponent, however this man had no knowledge of the technique and therefore was thrown with his own power. He slammed ungracefully into the ground and rolled.

The crowd of Japanese onlookers, who had been watching with sweaty palms roared, "Waaaaa!" However, Maeda's opponent was an American wrester and when Butcher Boy got up he looked very annoyed and charged in again. This time Maeda threw him with Tomoe Nage, and Butcher Boy flew over Maeda's head. However, Butcher was able to rotate his body to the side, so he landed on his shoulder. In a great scramble he got back to his feet. Maeda got hold of one of his sleeves and yanked on it two or three times before attacking with Uki Waza. The application was a little rough, but his opponent was thrown dramatically. All 30 Kan of the Butcher were thrown to the ground, however since he had spent many years training wrestling his body was hardly that of a normal person. Further, since Maeda had not struck a Kyusho, vital point, and his shoulders had not touched the mat, the Butcher rolled deftly onto his feet and stood back up almost as soon as the throw was finished.

Maeda thought about the problem. It was going to be hard to get both his shoulders on the ground at the same time. If he went down to the mats with Butcher, who was an expert at all forms of wrestling, and did poorly, Maeda might end up getting his shoulders pinned to the ground. Maeda couldn't let his guard down. In the end, he threw the Butcher three times, using powerful techniques, in order to put some fear in him. There was no way Maeda was going to charge right at him. Maeda breathed in, looking for an opening. Suddenly, Butcher Boy crouched his long body low, arching his back like a cat. He edged forward slowly, with a crafty look in his eye. At first Maeda instinctively protected his groin, but soon realized he needn't worry about that. His opponent was slowly approaching in his low stance, his long arms quivering like they were seeking prey. Then Maeda saw it. Butcher was going to try and scoop up his legs! Very well, now he was ready. At that moment Butcher Boy darted forward as fast as a rabbit fleeing a trap, seeking Maeda's legs. Maeda slipped deftly aside and, Butcher Boy grabbed Maeda's neck, setting up for a Koshi Nage, hip throw.

The absolute gall of this man! Attacking with this bungling Koshi Waza! It was like a moth flying into a flame. Maeda immediately shifted his hips around, setting himself up and hurtled Butcher Boy to the ground in a violent throw. Butcher Boy, now in a panic, kept his grip on Maeda's collar. Maeda, unable to resist, was pulled down on top of him. In a moment, Butcher Boy's both shoulders were flat against the ground. The referee shouted, "That's a pin!" Maeda had a definitive win. He was not at all expecting to win in that fashion. The Japanese in attendance had gone wild clapping, shouting and cheering.

After a ten-minute break the second bout began. This time Butcher Boy definitely had a bit of fear in him, and he did not attack with the ferocious intensity of before. Instead, he would drop to one knee and go for Maeda's legs with those fearsomely long arms. It unnerved Maeda, reminding him of how opponents would aim for the groin when doing Gekken, sword sparring.[58] However, once he dropped down and made his attack, he didn't continue to advance, but waited. Maeda kept switching his front leg and back leg around preparing himself to step on a drawn sword, though he was of half a

---

[58] 撃剣 Gekken, also called Gekiken, that emerged in the post-Meiji Restoration (1868) Era. Generally speaking, it was a precursor to Kendo that was a more rough and tumble since you were allowed to grab or trip your opponent. The fighters were often former sword instructors to Samurai, who now found themselves unemployed. The format of the bouts was similar to Sumo, in the sense that the fighters were divided into East and West and they were ranked. Each person fought with their own style.

Maeda's comment is interesting as it gives us a glimpse into how rough those bouts were even in the mid-Meiji era when he was in university.

mind just to continue escaping.[59] At any rate, it seemed quite clear that Butcher Boy was going to get hold of his leg. Since Maeda understood his opponent's intent, he kept his hips low and a firm grip on his sleeves. Butcher Boy did a thorough job of blocking Maeda's hands.

Maeda turned as he yanked hard on his opponent's sleeves. Butcher Boy followed him around but stayed with one knee planted on the ground. The sight of him dragging one knee along the ground seemed grotesque to Maeda but Butcher Boy seemed unconcerned. Maeda kept expecting him to stand up at any moment, but he didn't. Maeda put his hips in deep and attacked with Tsurikomi Goshi, since his opponent was such a large man. They fell as one with Maeda on top. The ground reverberated with the shock of the two men striking the ground, Maeda's opponent being almost twice as heavy as he. The Japanese watching felt a cold chill go down their spines as they dreaded what might come next.

However, Maeda had come up with a plan and falling to the ground together had been part of it. Since he was on top he attacked with Kuzure Kesa-gatame. He gripped both Butcher Boy's sleeves and extended both of his arms as much as he could, while forcing his body down, trying to pin the man. However, his right hand slipped off and Butcher Boy used that chance to roll his body so he was in a crawl position. This man was an expert at steadily moving his body forward across an opponent, so Maeda leapt up making his opponent rise into a squat. As he stood Maeda took his arm in an elbow lock. Having managed to take Butcher Boy's arm he wanted to make the most of this chance before his opponent could react, so he locked the elbow hard. Butcher Boy tried to escape in the opposite direction, twisting his body, but his body wouldn't endure it and a *Bokkiri!* popping sound came from his elbow.

With a sigh of relief, Maeda released the man's arm and Butcher Boy sank to the ground, crying out that he surrendered. The spectators were in an uproar and even Maeda became worried about

---

[59] *Hakujin Fumubeshi* 白刃踏むべし *Hakujin* means drawn blade and *Fumu* means to step on. The saying refers to being so utterly committed to a duel that you will step on a live blade (in order to achieve victory.)

the man's predicament. Upon closer inspection, Butcher Boy's face had gone pale and he couldn't move his arm. Tears were streaming down his face. As his arm got inspected Maeda couldn't decide if the situation was wretched or comical. The arm wasn't broken, and the joint wasn't dislocated, the tendons had just been stretched and he couldn't move his arm. Since this was a "best of three" duel, Maeda had taken the day, and it seemed Butcher Boy was in no position to dispute that. The duel had been short since the first round lasted 8 minutes and 10 seconds and the second round lasted only 3 minutes and 15 seconds.

While at long last Maeda felt satisfied with his victory, the Americans in attendance were grumbling and looking unsatisfied. Their mean-spirited comments showed no sign abating, even go as far as to make foolish comments like, "There is no way that was an honest win, no one can win that fast." Maeda thought they should go over and talk to Butcher Boy who was still unable to move his arm and was busy feeling sorry for himself. Looking at it from the perspective on one who is introducing Judo, no doubt the bout just witnessed would be bewildering to the uninitiated. While a victory was a victory Maeda felt unsatisfied. Be that as it may he was becoming known as Hyakusen-Hyakusho, a man who fights a hundred battles, and wins a hundred battles. However, like today, some opponents may view him as an easy mark, like a cat toying with a mouse. In the end, this turned out to be Maeda's first public duel since he arrived in America. The people that had shamelessly derided him will now have to clean up the mess they made.

Thinking back on the match, under normal conditions even if Butcher Boy had succeeded in scooping up both Maeda's legs, causing him to land flat on his back, it wouldn't have been a big deal. That was something that happened in duels, however it was one of the conditions of the fight and it cannot be undone now. Since Maeda was in a hurry to win, he made use of that condition.

The Americans continued to complain amongst themselves as they slowly filed out, while the Japanese, who comprised over half of the spectators, were overjoyed, pushing into Maeda's break room. They were all wild with glee and thanked Maeda for winning. As a result of this, membership in the Dojo increased.

Time passed and July turned to August. The winter in New York is cold and the summer is hot. So hot, in fact, that Maeda who did not handle heat well, felt his bones would melt. The wealthy had brought their families to the beach. For the most part workers spent the afternoon at Coney Island or Manhattan Beach. Particularly on Sunday, the crowds were huge and the duel at Manhattan Beach had served as a huge advertisement, quickly elevating Maeda's name after word of his victory spread.

第七勝 *Dainanasho*
Seventh Victory

Sumo, Kento Ryodo no Kyoryokumono
A Strong Man, Both a Wrestler and Boxer

Bathers at Manhattan Beach, NY. 1905

Bathers at Omori Beach, Tokyo 1905

The positioning of Coney Island and Manhattan Beach relative to New York City somewhat resembles how Omori beach is situated in relation to Tokyo. However, Manhattan Beach is not a dirty beach like Omori is. The white sand and clean air make a wonderful place to bathe in the ocean. Innumerable people go in and out of the ocean, and vendors pack the sidewalk along with many sideshows and nicknack shops. It is always bustling, from noon until midnight. Maeda had been staying in this area and teaching Judo until the end of August.

One day another person appeared answering Maeda's challenge. He was both a champion boxer and champion wrestler from Boston. His name was Meyer. Maeda guessed that Meyer was of mid-level weight, which meant mid-level amongst other wrestlers. From Maeda's perspective he was one step up in size. When Meyer saw how small Maeda was, he immediately began to act condescending as if saying, "I could knock this little Jap down with one punch." He proceeded to make an offer, "Let's bet $300!" Maeda responded by saying, "I'm not interested in gambling, if anyone is interested in challenging me as a test of who is stronger, I'm game." Judging by the look on Meyer's face the man was not satisfied with this answer and started mumbling something.

In fact, Maeda was neither for nor against placing a bet on a fight, even if he lost he was not honor bound to New York and he would not hesitate to bet it all, placing his life on the line. However, the fact was, at the time he was poor. Not poor like he couldn't afford a car, he couldn't even afford train fare, which limited his freedom of movement. Thus, he had no money to bet. If the money was going to a duel and he would get some part of it even if he were defeated, Maeda was more than willing to put money on the line. However, the first step was for both parties to place their money on the table and sign a contract, which Maeda wasn't able to do.

"Frankly, I am confident enough in my abilities to bet on myself, however I, personally, am not interested in betting, let me ask you to come again tomorrow, giving me time to think about the conditions of the duel and ready myself to be your opponent in this bet." Maeda said seeking to put off the contract for a day. Just then a Japanese man with whom he had been previously conferring stepped over. He was an acquaintance of Maeda from the Japanese Village. The man said, "Actually, if you are looking for a person to place a bet, I will do it."

Maeda was energized by this announcement however his would-be opponent Meyer seemed to withdraw a bit, looking hesitant. Maeda's acquaintance looked askance at Meyer and added, "I will take any bet of this sort, if you are willing to settle this now we can." And with that he reached into his breast pocket for his wallet. As it turned out, Meyer, who had been supremely confident up until this point, actually had no money on him. He mumbled and fumbled with excuses but was deflated. Finally, Meyer leaned close to the Japanese man and whispered something in his ear. Eventually, Meyer turned back to Maeda and said with feigned innocence, "This man and I have come to terms regarding the bet, so you and I only need to make the terms of the bout."

Maeda set forth the same conditions as the bout from the other day: both parties wear Keikogi, if thrown it only counts as a win if both shoulders touch the mats, Gyaku and Shime will be done until the opponent signals defeat. Meyer agreed to these terms and both parties signed the document. Now Maeda's opponent couldn't get away.

The day of the match arrived. All around there were American and Japanese flags flying. The referee and the timer, who announced when five minutes and when ten minutes had passed, found their spots. The many Japanese and American spectators found their seats and the man in charge of starting the match shouted, "Time!" and the match began. Maeda and Meyer moved to the center of the mats and shook hands, before stepping back. They then began to slowly advance on one another before grabbing each other's Keikogi.

Initially, Meyer, who was used to wrestling and boxing, put all his power into his attacks. On the other hand, Maeda had no idea how his opponent was going to attack, or what techniques he would use, so he maintained Shizentai, a relaxed natural stance, ready for anything. On one hand you had a man who was one step higher in size, pushing and pulling with all his might, and on the other side you had a smaller Japanese man, who was standing passively in a natural stance, with his mouth open like he was staring at a tiger in a cage. Quite an unusual contrast.

With a shout of *Ya!* Meyer, the man from Boston who was both a champion boxer and a champion wrestler, charged in to crush the tiny Jap in one squeeze of his fist. This is something that Judoka never do. Maeda wondered why foreigners always seemed to have weak hips. When training do they focus all their strength in their shoulders and therefore forget about their hips? Or are they just naturally predisposed to not developing strong hips? No matter what the answer is, such people are easy to manage when they leap in. Rather than a Sutemi Waza, Maeda attacked with a Koshi Waza and threw him to the ground, hard enough to rattle the man. Meyer got up and Maeda threw Meyer several more times, tumbling his giant body all over the mats, much to the relief of the assembled Japanese spectators.

Meyer, when compared with Butcher Boy, was a much easier opponent to deal with and Maeda decided to simply throw him down as many times as he wanted. A small man sending a large man tumbling down to the ground was quite gratifying and not particularly taxing. Those watching would enjoy a dramatic spectacle. However, as Meyer was an experienced wrestler, he was well versed in being thrown and he rolled smoothly back to his feet without both shoulders touching the mats and charged in again. Having been thrown several times he was getting more than a little embarrassed at how he was losing face, which lit a fire in him. He gradually became rougher and desperate. One punch of his to the jaw or eye and Maeda might not be able to recover. However, Meyer seemed to be out of breath and getting tired and looked as if the tide of battle was in Maeda's favor. He grabbed both of Meyer's sleeves and attacked with Tsurikomi Goshi, falling on top of him as he threw.

The foreigners in attendance, seeing the two fall together, thought that this was good for their side, so they started clapping and cheering. However, Maeda immediately made use of the situation and, keeping hold of Meyer's sleeves extended his arms as far as he could out to the sides as he pressed down in a Kesa-gatame, easily causing Meyer's shoulders to press to the mats. The referee shouted out, "That's a pin!" The first round was a clear and easy win by Maeda. The time was 3 minutes and 12 seconds.

After a ten-minute break the second round began. This time Meyer was noticeably calmer, and in fact seemed subdued. Maybe because he had lost a big point, maybe because he was a bit afraid, but he was keeping his distance and not attacking. It was easy for Maeda to respond to this man's attacks, however an opponent with a firm guard who wouldn't attack was the most dangerous type of opponent for Maeda. For a while they both glared at each other, however Maeda saw that his hips were out too far, like he was getting ready to sit down on the toilet, so he quickly snatched both sleeves.

Having seized his sleeves, Maeda had taken control of the situation. At first he thought about Tomoe Nage, however if the opponent didn't stand up, it would be impossible to employ. He used his sleeves to pull him first forward then around in a circle, which must have been embarrassing for him. Meyer struggled as he was being pulled around, eventually raising his upper body. Seeing this moment Maeda thought, "Ippon!" and threw with a textbook Tomoe Nage. Meyer traced a huge half circle before crashing to the ground. His opponent was not unfamiliar with being thrown and as he flew through the air he twisted his body do he ended up on all fours.

Being on all fours like this was the safest position for American wrestler and the easiest to defend from. No matter how he was thrown, both shoulders would never touch the ground. However, just as he thought he was safe Maeda mounted him like a horse from behind and use Okuri Eri to choke him. The choke was good, but Meyer would not signal his defeat. The Japanese watching the event cheered at the choke, shouting "That's a choke! You're done!" Maeda also realized he was almost there. He wrapped his legs around Meyer's abdomen as he kept up with the choke and pushed his body forward. He gave a final squeeze with all his strength and Meyer couldn't take it anymore. With a gurgling sound from his throat, he went limp.

The Japanese spectators had never seen a person brought down with a choke and were thunderstruck, suddenly the mood of the crowd shifted and they stood up shouting, "Waaa! Is he dead?! This is terrible! Let him go!" The referee just stood there swaying. Maeda thought the whole scene bizarre and slowly released his grip while lifting Meyer up. Maeda used the palm of his hand to strike Meyer in a certain spot in the center of the back, a resuscitation technique called Ikkatsu. and Meyer's eyes fluttered open, and he suddenly slapped the mats with both hands several times while shouting, "I give!" It was almost a comedy scene.

This round had taken less than two minutes beginning to end, and Maeda had easily and cleverly won the bout. Meyer paid the $300 to a certain Japanese man and went back to feeling sorry for himself.⁶⁰

⁶⁰ This diagram from Inoguchi Yoshitame's 1912 book *Randori and Resuscitation: A Jujutsu Textbook* 乱捕活法柔術教科 shows various Kyusho, vital points that can be used for either causing injury or reviving a person. The spot on the back indicated by the arrow is used for reviving someone who passes out from a choke.

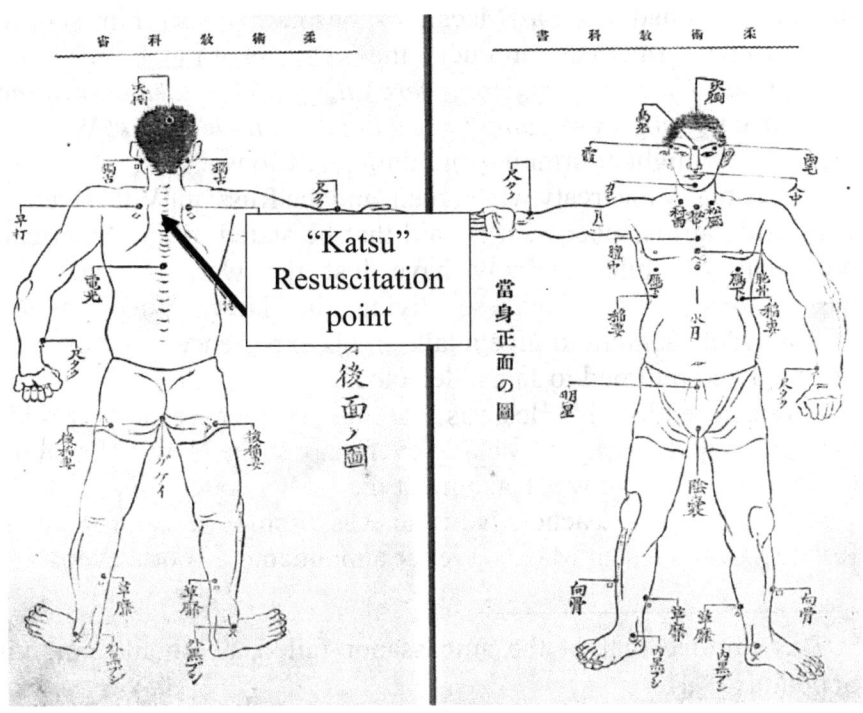

第八勝 *Daihassho*
Eighth Victory

Ikyo no Kigu
Surprise Meeting in a Strange Land

Before long it was September, and the weather became much cooler. Day by day the vacationers left. Around that time the newspapers all carried stories of the Japanese-Russian peace accord being negotiated in Portsmouth, Maine. Every day the papers carried pictures of Ambassador Komura and Count Sergius Witte, with a detailed description of their movements and their statements. No matter where he went Maeda found everyone was discussing these negotiations. The Japanese living in New York were vigorous in stating their opinions, often speaking in praise of Ambassador Komura. These Japanese people also added that if he were to sign an unfavorable and insulting treaty, they would flat out kill him. There was even one man who sent a package that contained a Tanto, short sword, to the ambassador, causing quite a commotion.[61] Since the men who had acted as Maeda's sponsors had seen him submit two different Americans in duels, they were very much puffed up with pride. *The Americans that were attempting to take everything and leave nothing were going to be stopped in their tracks!* Was the theme every night at drinking and dining sessions.

Eventually the treaty was signed, and the Russian Witte swelled with pride at his success. It is said that he stated to the American politicians, "While we may have lost the war, we won the negotiations." The Japanese living in New York invited Ambassador Komura to give a talk on his experiences, however he declined and returned to Japan dejected.

Maeda ended his lessons at the summer resort in mid-September and he began teaching every day at the New York Dojo. Previously, when he was teaching at the YMCA one of his students was a gymnastics teacher. Now he was running a youth club in Rockport and he sent Maeda a letter announcing a sports event and

---

[61] This implied that, if the ambassador failed, he should commit Seppuku.

inviting him to attend. Madea took the letter and visited Tomita Rokudan. Tomita had previously moved to Newport however recently he had returned to Columbia University where he was working with Professor Tanitsu on his research into aquatic species. Having met Tomita Rokudan after being separated for a time, they both travelled to Rockport, which they could get to in a day.

The pair arrived in the evening, just as the sports event was starting, so they immediately began their demonstration. As usual, Tomita Rokudan was one applying the techniques and Maeda was the one receiving the techniques and being thrown. Then, Maeda trained with several of the stronger youths. While the session was ostensibly about "training" the youths were clearly putting everything they had into the session, hoping against hope to get a point on Maeda. So, the "training" was basically the same thing as duel at this point. However, Maeda had become used to such a situation and he easily handled his opponents, tumbling them about like balls until they became woozy. It was a good session he submitted the stronger ones with chokes or joint locks, none of which broke any bones. Since there were none of the typical conditions that were common in bouts, Maeda felt he could move freely.

That evening Maeda was staying in the apartment over the youth club. As he was opening the door to his room, an American man greeted him. "Two years ago, I was in Tokyo and trained with you several times at the Kodokan. You are my Sensei." he said appreciatively. Maeda was able to make the connection. This was the first time a person from another country had ever spoken such kind words to him. In truth, it made him feel homesick. The next day the American took him on a tour of Niagara Falls. American's claim it is the largest in the world, and it is quite impressive indeed. Being treated warmly while being taken on a sightseeing tour was a happy time for Maeda.

The next day Maeda took his leave from the youth club and returned to New York. The very next day he returned to teaching at the Dojo as normal. Later he received a letter form Ono Sandan who had travelled to the southern part of the United States. "The other day I completely dominated a larger opponent in a duel! A second match is scheduled soon!" Maeda was thrilled by this news and eagerly awaited a letter bearing good news. However, a few days an unfortunate letter arrived, the second bout was marred by the referee ignoring the rules of the match and siding with Ono's opponent. Ono Sandan was defeated.

大野三段の災難 *Ono Sandan no Sainan*
Ono Sandan Encounters Disaster

The Japanese students studying at Yale university returned from their trip to the south and told what they had seen. During the bout, Ono Sandan's opponent grabbed his Keikogi and then immediately head-butted Ono Sandan in the face. Then grabbed Ono's fingers, which were holding his Keikogi and tried to break them. Ono's opponent continued with innumerable violations. However, Ono continued to abide by the rules of the match and tried to engage his opponent.

It goes without saying that those acts of viciousness were in violation of the rules, clearly the referee and the opponent's manager should be working to stop this. However, they had obviously pressed cash into the hands of the patrolman standing on the side, supervising the event, and he had ignored all of it. Three of Ono Sandan's Japanese friends who had been watching the fight, moved towards the ring protesting vigorously, however the police officer who was a giant of a man, bigger than Hitachiyama escorted them out of the facility, and that was the end of it. In the end their protests were for naught.

During all this, Ono Sandan's opponent struck him in the face again, and Ono's face swelled up so much he couldn't even see, so it became impossible for him to continue the fight. They said that Ono Sandan had been able to throw the man one or two times. Maeda thought that if Ono had found a chance to attack with a throw he should have then gone to the ground with the opponent and sought to pin him. Barring that, a Gyaku or Shime. If that too failed, he should have simply resorted to a full-on fight and punched and kicked his way through it, at any rate going all in. However, he wasn't there at the time and didn't know the full story, at any rate a sorry situation.

Since Ono Sandan was unable to continue, it went without saying that he was the loser in that duel. In reality, it was his American opponent, who had violated the terms of the match by head-butting, should have been declared the loser by a just referee, but they were all aligned against Ono Sandan who was trapped in an impossible situation.

As it turned out Ono Sandan had completely dominated his opponent in their first meeting the previous day. For the second bout, the following day, the public match had drawn a lot of attention from the public, including upper class gentlemen, most of whom had bet money on the Judoka. On the other hand, the workers and other lower-class people had bet their money on the American. Thus, when the American was announced the winner, the gentlemen declared the match unfair and began protesting loudly. In response the working-class people rose up in unison and a huge shouting match ensued. Outnumbered, the gentleman let the matter lie. In other words the lower-class spectators had bribed the referee and other officials.

The next day the upper crust of the town, including the mayor, took Ono with them to arrest the violent opponent from the previous night's bout. Their intention was to take him to court and the gentlemen stated their intention to stand as witnesses for Ono and they even went so far as to send Ono a consolation letter. As it turned out all this was for naught as the cowardly man had fled in the night to another state.

Ono Sandan had not yet gotten used to how such duels can go, and he was unfamiliar with the local customs. It wasn't until later he realized that the official looking document that was signed by the mayor of the town and other persons was just an apology for what happened and not worth anything. If they had truly been on Ono's side, they would have stopped the illegal match last night and immediately arrested the man and thrown him in jail so he couldn't escape. This completely exposed the true soul of America for what it was, a barbarian country that was barely policed like it was still a frontier country.

Indeed, the day after that, all the newspapers were unified in their support of Ono however this only amounted to a pittance. The following day however, the front pages all talked about how Ono had clearly lost. Even today Ono Sandan's left eyeball is still in bad shape.

Two or three days later, even those that had initially supported Ono began to say disparaging things like, "How come when your opponent started breaking the rules, you didn't defend yourself properly. It seems part of the reason you got injured is that you didn't fight back." So, though Ono acted honorably and by the rules like a gentleman, without never broke any, it only resulted in him receiving an injury.

A Japanese man, who shall go unnamed, accompanying Ono Sandan stopped by Washington DC on his way north to lodge a protest at the Japanese embassy. He explained what had happened and asked if there was anything the embassy could to alleviate the fury they felt. The embassy representative he talked to responded that the embassy could not make this an international incident and therefore cannot get involved, however he personally would try to assist in any way he could. This statement was made by a high-level secretary at the time.

復讎進軍 *Fukushu Shingun*
The Group Set Off to Seek Revenge

As it turned out the story of this meeting at the Japanese embassy made the news. "After a match in a certain southern state a Japanese Judoka complained to the Japanese embassy over unfair treatment by his opponent, claiming that the southern area of Ashville, North Carolina is completely out of government control and that anyone entering that area should be cautioned." Further, a certain Chicago based newspaper ran a scathing article stating, "Getting injured in the course of a fight goes with the territory and is hardly something to contact the Japanese embassy over."

If things had gone as they should, Ono Sandan would have never had a duel with that man, one who behaved in such a cowardly way. Having won, he stuffed all the money in his pocket. If Judoka do not pay attention during duels, a victory will end up turning into a defeat and you will end up seriously injured. Someone who is a coward will pretend everything is an accident, striking you in the stomach with his knee, or moving like sparks flying off a rock hit with a sword, shoving a finger into your eye or nose. The most extreme case is while you are trying to apply a choke, your opponent grabs and squeezes your testicles. It seems the only recourse to prevent this is to wear the stiff Fundoshi loincloth favored by Sumo wrestlers in Japan, and then wear Sarumata "monkey pants" shorts above that. This is why the Fundoshi is tied tightly.

There are people that go to even greater extremes, for example stuffing poison under their nails and then scratching you. Several days later these simple scratches turn into a terrible wound. Initially you won't detect such cunning, thinking that because you are acting properly your opponent isn't planning to do something awful. Maeda occasionally encountered such trickery, so he made a habit of checking out his opponent before the duel.

Getting injured by accident during a match is just something that happens and can't be helped, however that doesn't mean you shouldn't pay attention. If your opponent makes a ham-fisted attempt to cheat, the audience will pick up on it and condemn it and a trustworthy referee will declare him the loser. Be that as it may, Maeda, when reflecting on his experiences said, even if you are being cautious with your attacks, never let your guard down and this will protect you from disaster.

There seemed to be no recourse for Ono and his friends, which had them furious. Thus, it is important to choose the referee carefully, since there are quite a few that will ty and deceive you. Money is the root of evil for Americans.

Sometime later, another message from Ono Sandan arrived addressed to Maeda. "The other day as I was recovering from my injury, the guy I fought re-appeared in the area and after talking with various people came to me and apologized.

What he said was along the lines of, "Regarding the match the other day, I realize a lot of people bet money on me, so I had to do everything I could to win." He then went on to say, rather stiffly, that he would split the money with me. "Since I let my greed get the better of me, I wish to apologize from the bottom of my heart." He said, asking for forgiveness. Ono added as a final note, "While on the outside I shook hands and showed that we had resolved the situation peacefully, on the inside I was only thinking of revenge."

As it turned out the American added, "One night I would like to do a wrestling and Judo demonstration with all the money going towards defraying Ono Sandan's medical costs." This plan appealed to Ono Sandan though he would be unable to do a Judo demonstration on his own. Since he would be travelling to New

York in the next couple of days he would try and see if some arrangement could be made.

After arriving in New York and talking with Maeda about it, Maeda agreed to accompany Ono and the two set out. Even then, half of Ono Sandan's face was swollen and his left eye was only half open. Clearly, he had taken a beating. Ono was a large man who had put his time in at the Kodokan and yet his opponent had been much larger man, covered with muscles. Despite being head-butted by that man, Ono had continued because he believed his body would allow him to overcome anything. He even commented in a jocular manner, "I wanted to know which was stronger, his head or my face."

Ono had stayed in New York for a few days before heading south with Maeda. However, when they arrived there was no sign of the demonstration taking place that day or in the near future. On the other hand, various wrestlers in that area were continuing to do matches in front of crowds as before. It seemed as if the talk of doing a joint demonstration had fallen by the wayside. Ono's desire for revenge was now front and center in his mind and Maeda was now realizing that paying money to take the train here was not working out as he had expected. With the two feeling like they had been duped they got a hold of some people they were familiar with in the area and had a talk.

The plan for a joint exhibition and demonstration had indeed fallen by the wayside. Not content to let the matter lie, Maeda found a translator to discuss the matter with one of the local men. That man shrugged off the cancellation by saying, "I don't think it's actually been cancelled, it's just that the demonstration hall is closed." He added, "It is too bad you came all this way, but since you are here are you interested in doing a duel American-style without Keikogi? Since news of Mr. Ono's defeat was in the newspapers, it is unlikely that a Judo demonstration will attract any paying spectators."

The answer clearly showed that the man thought he was an idiot. Similarly, the Japanese man serving as an interpreter was a man who had married an American woman and clearly thought that everyone else was beneath his nose. Not exactly a person who could be relied on, and now the situation was not progressing ideally. A Judo Sensei couldn't wait for two or three weeks for the situation to change, that would be like hanging himself out to dry, so, seeing no other way, he approached the local man and said, "I am fine with wrestling without a Keikogi, find me an appropriate opponent." However, the man replied that he wouldn't be able to find an opponent right away. Hearing this Maeda said in a voice that made it clear he was ready to fight, "Then bring the guy that Ono fought the other day." The man demurred saying, "Well, that guy said he would never fight wearing a Judo Keikogi again." Maeda replied, "That's why I said that I would wrestle American-style with no Keikogi." The conversation seemed to be going in circles, then the man admitted, "The other night he got into a fight and got stabbed in the leg, he will be in the hospital for some time." Clearly this was a dead-end.

The pair were spoiling for a duel but there was nothing to be done about it. They decided to cure their frustration by teaching at the local YMCA. The grandfather of one of the students at the YMCA asked Maeda and Ono if they would do a Judo demonstration and lecture that evening at a local athletic club. While Maeda was just coming off an idiotic negotiation and now was being asked to do what amounted to unpaid volunteer work, he realized that he had travelled a long way to get to this place so turning around and heading home without doing a demonstration would only compound his loss. With that new frame of mind, he and Ono set off to do the demonstration. They showed four or five Kata and, since this whole trip was going to end without a clear resolution, they decided to go all out for their final demonstration and really show the crowd something. Maeda and Ono conferred and threw everything they had into the Kata. As it turned out the demonstration went spectacularly well and the crowd cheered wildly. Later they were treated to a fine meal.

However, no one volunteered to train during the demonstration. Upon returning to their rooming house, the two threw various plans back and forth at each other but they realized one of the main problems was the language barrier. Since they didn't speak the language, they were effectively mute.

Fortunately, it turned out there was an elementary school art teacher staying in the same rooming house. He was incredibly friendly and told them about how he worked at two different elementary schools and was very busy all the time. That being said, he was more than willing to teach the two English. Maeda thought that this was a lucky break indeed and they began studying for two hours every day. He made them read aloud and, quite unexpectedly, they found themselves progressing nicely. The American elementary school teacher's method was quite clever and after a short amount of time the men felt, to a degree, they could figure out what other people were saying.

While Maeda recommended that Ono return to New York, Maeda decided to stay in the area and find an opponent, or perhaps find a way to gather some students as he continued his English lessons. The truth was, they were having trouble gathering the funds to pay for both of them to travel at the same time, thus Ono Sandan was thinking seriously of heading back to New York first. Maeda, who was able to make himself understood to a degree while walking around town, using only words and short phrases had decided to stay. Ono Sandan finally made his decision and announced it to Maeda, "I'm sorry you got dragged into this, I dragged you down here without much planning and look how it ended up. There is no excuse for my lack of foresight. I am embarrassed to be returning to return to the big city and leaving you here in this barbarian land completely devoid of police protection. But being unable to communicate I am of no use to you here. I'm sorry but I will leave you to your language study and return to New York." The two had a drink celebrate their decisions.

Ono Sandan returned to New York and Maeda stayed on, however he soon found himself lonely. He had been confident he was gaining in language ability only to find he wasn't being understood when he went out into town. Eventually he couldn't bear it anymore and began to long to return to New York. However, money was a problem and he found himself orphaned and in a very dark mood indeed. Thinking "Well there is nothing to be done about it now, best to sleep on it." He lay down for a mid-day nap. Just then, the manager who had been part of the recent duel fought by Ono appeared and asked Maeda if he was interested in a bout. Maeda felt like he was in a dream and sprang into action.

第九勝 *Daikyusho*
Ninth Victory

大野三段の復讐 *Ono Sandan no Fukushu*
The Revenge of Ono Sandan

Downtown Atlanta, Early 1900's

The man who was looking for a duel was an American Catch-as-catch-can wrestler. The place was in the biggest city in the south, a city called Atlanta. The negotiations were legitimate. After what seemed like an eternity, Maeda felt human again and immediately agreed to the terms.

After talking to the manager two or three times, Maeda broached the subject of the man Ono had dueled with. He wanted to train with the man as a test of strength, albeit not in a public forum, but just as practice. He flattered the manager profusely and he eventually agreed to have the man train with Maeda while wearing a Keikogi. So, Maeda had a one-off training session with the man. He weighed about the same as Ono Sandan. Maeda wasn't sure if the man had fallen on hard times or what, but for such a well-known wrestler he seemed weak, and Maeda threw him around like a ragdoll.

Later, when they talked, the man said that Ono Sandan had been dueling at a leisurely pace and he had become flustered, so he had struck Ono in the face with a wild head-butt, and for the injuries incurred he expressed sympathy. The man turned to Maeda and flat out said that while Ono Sandan was very strong he added, "That man wasn't used to duels. I have done a lot of rough things to win the money that was on the line, and I don't think he deserved to get hurt so bad, however him trying to go slow was a detriment to me. Anyone would do what I did in that situation. Other guys that wrestle are far more violent than I am. When guys in the wrestling world have a duel, what happened the other day can be the line between winning and defeat." Though he said this calmly, his face told a different story. Maeda challenged him to a public duel, but he refused. For his part, Maeda's anger had been assuaged after having thrown him hither and yon. The man said his name was Charlie Olsen. [62]

---

[62] Left: Charles Cutler, born Charles Olsen (1884 ~ 1952.) in 1908. Right: "Olsen demonstrating full Nelson on training partner."

OLSEN DEMONSTRATING FULL NELSON ON TRAINING PARTNER.

In the future, Ono Sandan would occasionally interact with European wrestlers and even when wrestling without a Keikogi, he wouldn't lose as bad as he did with Olsen. He simply was not used to how duels worked at this point.

Maeda arrived in Atlanta. First, he went to a local athletic club and negotiated terms for a Judo demonstration. At this point Maeda took the fact that it would end in a duel as a foregone conclusion. The club was delighted and immediately agreed to the terms. Thanks to the club, Maeda would have enough money to pay for his hotel stay until the match. Since the match was a few days away and sitting alone in his hotel room was boring he went walking downtown. When the locals saw him, they stopped and stared, saying, "There is a China-man coming." There wasn't a single Japanese person in Atlanta, and anyone colored like an east Asian person was considered "Chinese." Maeda did not care for this at all, however as both the demonstration at the local athletic club, as well as news of his upcoming bout had been reported in the paper and even featured a picture of Maeda, he was bound to be recognized.

The title of the article was "A True Japanese Judoka Has Arrived!" In typical American fashion the locals were eager to see something new and different so whenever Maeda entered a restaurant or other shop, he felt that people were sizing him up. They then peppered Maeda with so many questions he felt like it was May when the cicadas first appear and fill the air with angry noises. If he answered, then they followed up with a stream of questions which Maeda felt was intolerable. The more people that talked to him the more tight-lipped he became.

There was another matter that began to cause him consternation. On the day before the duel his tooth started giving him trouble. The pain was excruciating and the moment it seemed to abate, it rebounded again with a vengeance. On top of this, the couple staying in the room beside Maeda were newlyweds from the countryside who were staying in Atlanta on their honeymoon. First, they were kissing then laughing and making a racket, finally there was the sound of crying. In short, while Maeda was straining to endure the pain in his mouth, he was being serenaded by the racket in the next room. Finally, dawn broke, and he rushed to see a dentist to see if he could do anything for the pain. However, he was unable to chew and had to swallow his food whole like a cormorant. Considering how this made his stomach feel, the match tonight was in doubt.

However, if he cancelled the match, he would lose all the goodwill he had built up until now. Maeda spent the day in a daze. Eventually evening arrived and he walked over to where the event was being held and he found that his opponent had rejected wearing a Keikogi. Wrestling "naked" already put Maeda at a disadvantage and which would be compounded by the poor condition Maeda was in. Both parties negotiated and it was decided the first round would be Western style with no Keikogi and follow those rules. The next round both combatants would wear a Keikogi and fight according to Judo rules, however Shime and Gyaku would be off-limits, only throws. A throw wouldn't automatically result in a win and a fighter had to force both shoulders of his opponent to the ground to get a pin. According to the rules, if it was a draw after two rounds, the third round would be according to the rules favored by the person who won their round in the shortest time.

These rules certainly did not favor Maeda. It was going to be tough winning a duel against the American with Western-style rules, while "naked" without a Keikogi. His opponent was 4 Kan, 15 kilograms, heavier and Maeda had not trained in a long time, so he was beginning to feel like he was going to lose the match. On the other hand, if they were using Judo rules, Maeda felt he could drop his opponent in two or three minutes. For example, if it took his opponent 10 minutes to beat him with wrestling and it took Maeda only five minutes to beat him with Judo, then, according to the rules, the final round would be Judo-style and Maeda would almost certainly win in that situation.

第十勝 *Daijusho*
Tenth Victory

Seiyoryu no Sumo
Western-style Wrestling

  Maeda had calculated how he planned to win this match, though he had never really wrestled Western-style before, though he had seen it upon occasion. It seemed to him that he needed to avoid being put on the bottom and other than that, look for a chance to throw his opponent. It seemed unlikely Maeda would be able to defeat this man in wrestling, so his goal was to stave off being defeated as long as possible. He was prepared for a defensive strategy.

  At last, time was called, and both combatants shook hands in the center before backing away and beginning the match. This was completely unlike Japanese Sumo, which Maeda had done every year at Waseda University's sports festival, even winning the top prize. However American wrestling was completely unfamiliar and strange. His opponent sought to get a quick victory in less than a minute while Maeda was doing his best to escape. The wrestler used his arms exclusively to grab at Maeda's legs. It seemed as if he could follow through with a Judo throw, however it didn't occur to him.

  Eventually the man drew near and attacked Maeda by wrapping his arm around Maeda's neck while going for a Koshi Nage, and both of them fell to the ground. As he was trying to pin Maeda, Maeda shifted his hips out and threw the wrestler off before standing up. Next the man grabbed the sides of Maeda's belt from below. Maeda responded by dropping his left foot back and sinking down onto his knee before throwing with Shoi-Nage. Since the wrestler had pulled in close when attacking, the throw was beautiful. After that, the wrestler decided to give up on throws and focus exclusively on taking Maeda's legs. Maeda was able to skillfully avoid his first three attempts, however on the fourth try he feinted as if he were going to wrap up Maeda's neck, before rapidly scooping up Maeda's legs. Due to the man's size and strength Maeda was unable to block and he fell prey to a beautiful takedown.

  Falling was no problem, as long as both shoulders did not touch the ground at the same time. Maeda immediately flipped his body over and stood, however without a moment's hesitation the man crawled over and grabbed Maeda's left leg, pulling him down again. Maeda twisted so he was facing away and tried to pull his leg free, but the wrestler followed him persistently and wrapped Maeda up from behind. Maeda got on his hands and knees and the man tried to roll him over. If he succeeded, he would then follow up by trying to pin Maeda.

Maeda had been able to throw the man off twice before, so he felt confident he could handle him this time as well, however it proved impossible. The wrestler had a firm hold on Maeda's waist and the only thing that was going to work was charging in full power.

Maeda shook his waist free and tried to stand up from all fours, however the man would not let go. If this were Judo, Maeda would have simply rolled on his back and gone to work on his opponent. However, this was wrestling, so if both shoulders touch the ground, it would mean he was defeated. The two of them continued to struggle on all fours like they were in some kind of dogfight. It wasn't pretty, but the two of them struggled fiercely. Maeda focused all his attention on escaping and was beginning to flag when the timekeeper called out that ten minutes had elapsed. Maeda breathed a sigh of relief. When they finally switched to Judo-style, he felt absolutely confident he could win in less than 10 minutes.

While Maeda was feeling confident, he charged his opponent, bristling with fighting spirit and latched onto the wrestler's right side. Maeda got hold of the man's left arm and pulled while using his right leg to extend the man's left knee, all while trying to roll on top of his opponent. This curious technique was surprisingly effective, and the wrestler was pulled from a crawl position onto his back and his right shoulder was forced onto the mats. If Maeda had immediately continued for the pin he might have won, however he wasn't sure he had the strength and hesitated. The man then used his head to prevent his other shoulder from contacting the mat and rotated back over into a crawl. However, the man's arm had released its hold on Maeda's waist, so he rapidly stood up and put some distance between them.

Realizing his gambit had failed, the wrestler also got up. He then went for the legs again and Maeda defended by shoving off his shoulder with both hands, which seemed to frustrate the man mightily. His next attack was to charge right in and grab Maeda around the waist. Maeda blunted this attack with O-soto Gari, which served to dump the man onto his butt. Though he was squatting and had been half-way toppled he wrapped his arms around Maeda's leg, which meant they ended up on all fours in like they were in a dog fight. Maeda thought that this was getting tedious, but he also realized the danger.

His opponent finally realized that Maeda was only doing defense, so he attacked with renewed ferocity. There were frequent close calls, but Maeda was able to endure. Then the timekeeper called out that 10 minutes had passed for the second time. Maeda was pretty tired by this point and he had fended off his opponent's attacks enough. The man again launched an intense attack and managed to pull Maeda down and onto his back. When the referee shouted, "That's a pin!" 5 minutes and 12 seconds had since the start of the third 10-minute period, for a total time of 25 minutes 12 seconds. It had been quite a struggle. So, after a 10-minute break they would have another round Judo-style while wearing Kekogi. Maeda felt the relief of being able to fight on his own terms.

This second match would be a Judo-style bout and his American wrestler opponent seemed quite subdued. He had been intending to submit Maeda within the first five minutes of the initial match, however it had required 25 minutes. Since many of his techniques had been foiled, the wrestler realized he was up against an unexpectedly dangerous opponent. The wrestler now seemed a bit dejected after realizing he was facing an opponent in a Judo-style match and there was no clear avenue for him to win. Seeing his opponent's expression gave Maeda all the power he needed.

The timekeeper shouted that it was time to start the next match and both combatants moved to the center and shook hands. Maeda's plan of attack was to throw his opponent until he got tired then pin him. He grabbed the man's sleeves and first, in order to startle him, he decided to kick him over with a Tomoe Nage. When the wrestler got up, he attacked with Ashibarai. At this point, the Judoka was basically handling the wrestler like a toy. His opponent clearly felt the match was a foregone conclusion and had resigned himself to that. Thus, his attacks lacked enthusiasm and the wrestler came after Maeda's legs sullenly, like a dog mourning the loss of his family. However, since Maeda had a firm grip on his sleeves, the man's arms couldn't reach. The Keikogi was holding him fast like it was wire, and his range of movement was decreased by half.

Maeda thought he could do as many Sutemi Waza as he wanted. However, if he made a blunder, his opponent would be on him with his deft pinning technique. A dangerous prospect. So, after throwing him tumbling through the air with two or three Tomoe Nage in order to put fear into the wrestler, Maeda switched to Koshi waza and Ashi Waza and continued to throw the man down again and again. When he appeared to be getting tired, Maeda attacked with Tsurikomi Goshi and slammed him into the ground with ferocious power.

Maeda went down at the same time, landing on top of the wrestler and pushing his sleeves out to the sides. The wrestler tried to push his head back and raise his shoulders off the mats, however unlike when he was shirtless, he couldn't easily roll over. Maeda continued to press until the referee shouted, "That's a pin!" The time was 8 minutes and 15 seconds.

Each competitor had won one match so, according to the rules, the final match would be as Maeda liked, wearing a Judo-style Keikogi. However, his opponent was resigned, "There is no need to continue. There is no way I can win, so it will just end up with me being humiliated. Let's just declare that I lost." However, the spectators were having none of it. "What's the matter? Don't you have any backbone? This is an insult to those of us watching! A duel is all about fate, you have a duty to fight with all your might until you can't go on anymore! Then the match can stop!"

So there was nothing to be done but go on with the match. The pair took a 10-minute break and then began the third match. Maeda's opponent didn't bring much enthusiasm to the match and indeed appeared sheepish. On the other hand, this served to fuel Maeda and as soon as the match started, though his opponent was down on all fours, completely on the defensive. Since Shime and Gyaku were off limits, Maeda could only really grab hold of the man's Keikogi, which was basically like western wrestling. Not an easy prospect an one fraught with danger.

However, the American wrestler considered the outcome of the match a foregone conclusion, so his heart wasn't in it. Maeda grabbed his sleeves and yanked him hard before throwing him. When he was looking winded, Maeda took him down and pushed his sleeves out to the sides. The man hardly resisted and both shoulders soon touched the mat and after only 4 minutes and 2 seconds the referee shouted, "That's a pin!" Maeda had won a good clean match.

Later in the changing room, after his opponent had taken off all his clothes, he walked over to Maeda and shook his hand. "I want you to take a look at something, you really hurt me with all those throws." From his back down to the outside of his thighs was all red and the skin was coming off in places. "Your skin is weak, Japanese spend all day throwing each other so we don't get red like that." The man replied, "It really burns, I don't know if I can take this." To which Maeda offered, "Well I can spray some whiskey on it if you like?" The man didn't realize Maeda was joking and took him up on his offer, Maeda took whiskey in his mouth and sprayed it out like a mist from his mouth. The man couldn't take it and ran around yelling how much it hurt. Finally, he said, "Man, I am never going to wear a Keikogi in a match again. If you ever want to wrestle again though let me know, you will get beat ten times in one hour!" Maeda, realizing the man was crying into his sake cup retorted, "How many ten-minute sessions make up an hour on your watch? To beat me one time took almost thirty minutes! If you wanted to beat me ten times, it would take until tomorrow morning! You are just lucky you are 4 or 5 Kan heavier than me, if we weighed the same, I could put you in a Keikogi and throw you into submission fifteen times in an hour." The man laughed ironically and said in a jocular tone, "I wouldn't put a Keikogi on again for anything." In a manner that seemed to imply that they were now friends he said, "I am sure we will meet up again somewhere." He handed over his card which gave his name as Sam Marburger. What a stupid, stupid man....

Having completely dominated Marburger, Maeda felt at long last like his tension regarding coming to the southern United States had faded. He went back to his hotel and stretched out on the bed and went to sleep. He had just closed his eyes when some sort of racket started in the hotel. A big man was having some disagreement with the manager over his bill and was causing a scene. As it turns out it was Marburger, who was staying at the same hotel. He was venting his frustration at having lost to Maeda by slamming the manager's head into the wash basin. The lobby was in an uproar as the manager, who was bleeding from a cut on his head, had bit Marburger's hand and wouldn't let go. It looked like two dogs fighting. The bellboy and the other staff were in shock and didn't know what to do. Maeda couldn't just lay there doing nothing so he inserted himself between the two and settled things down. He even brought out a bottle of whiskey to smooth things over. The next morning, before Maeda was even awake, he heard the voice of Marburger and his companions outside his door, "Sayonara!" After that departing word, he set off for parts unknown.

Later when Maeda was reading the paper, he saw an ad that featured a melodramatic picture of Marburger who was apparently set to duel in Nashville. Maeda mused, "That guy would fight friends, brothers or parents for money." [63]

---

[63] Sam Marburger pictured in *The Indianapolis News* Wednesday February 14th 1906

A JUDO WARRIOR'S JOURNEY AROUND THE GLOBE・世界横行柔道武者修業

渡英談 *Toeidan*
Talk of Travelling to England

In December of Meiji 38, 1905, Maeda departed from Atlanta and headed to Selma City in the state of Alabama. At the YMCA in that city, he was able to gather 23 students, so for the time being he stayed there. Maeda placed challenges in the local newspaper however, possibly due to news of Marburger's defeat spreading, no one seemed to be inclined to take up his offer.

Thus Meiji 39, 1906, began and the season was heading towards spring. One day a letter arrived from his friends in New York. "We have been invited to travel to England. So, should we go or not? Please send your response quickly." Maeda's reply was basically a request, "If we are going first, check to see what the conditions of the contract are." Over the past month, Maeda had been spending his time frivolously in this uncharted land, trying to teach people who did not understand what the essence of Judo was. Since he had no attachment to this area, the opportunity to go to England seemed like a lucky break. He was overjoyed.

The next day a telegram came saying, "We should go right away." This was so unexpected that Maeda felt like birds were suddenly flying up from below him. He immediately sent a telegram in reply, "I will depart tomorrow morning." Maeda then told his students he was leaving, and the next morning took the train to New York, arriving safely 39 hours later. He immediately went to the Dojo and it turned out the conditions for the trip to England were not to his satisfaction and he declined the offer. Ono Sandan had however, decided to accept the offer. This was an unfortunate end to Maeda's trip, since he had been excited by this grand opportunity throughout the 39-hour train ride to New York.

As it turned out there were two other telegrams from Paris. Upon opening them Maeda received another jolt. The first message said, "Please come to Paris. Reply immediately, we will pay your travel expenses." The telegram even included the reply fee. When he looked at the date, he realized it was over a month old. Crushing the paper in his hands Maeda realized while he had been dragging his feet around in the southern US, he had completely missed this opportunity. Why hadn't someone opened it for him? Or passed the message on? It seemed like for some reason his recent absence from New York had resulted in everything in his life falling apart.

From New York, it only takes about a week to get to London or Paris however it was hard to find an opportunity to go. If you had wads of money in your breast pocket, you could certainly book passage easily and be standing on the deck waving grandly as you depart on your voyage, spending the intervening days on light amusements. However, a chance to travel to Europe and have your living expenses paid for is almost unheard of, and Maeda had missed two opportunities. With his trip to Europe aborted, Maeda returned to teaching lessons at the Dojo.

Maeda soon discovered that while he had been in the southern US, another Judoka and Kendoka had arrived from Japan. Both were youths from the Butokukai martial arts organization in Kyoto. They did not come over alone, rather they accompanied a famous American railway man named Harriman. He brought the Japanese men along so that they could teach his son, however Harriman's son was completely uninterested in training. The two were now occasionally doing demonstration lectures at universities as well as at events organized by Harriman's acquaintances. Maeda did two or three demonstrations with the men and also went to Columbia University.

For the first few months after arriving in New York, Harriman had covered the men's expenses, however the Japanese men soon fell out of touch with Harriman. Maeda wasn't sure what sort of contract was agreed to in the beginning, but knowing the casual off-handed manner of Americans who enjoy new and unusual things, Maeda surmised Harriman probably spontaneously invited the Japanese martial artists to accompany him back to America from Japan. The Japanese, for their part, had their steamship passage paid for, and when two or three other fellows were added, it was of no concern to them.

They had agreed to the journey casually, their reason for embarking being because "they wanted to go." Now it was hard for them to complain about their situation. If they were promised jobs as teachers, then they should have requested a contract to that effect. In addition to these two, there were also a few others Japanese men that were around 22 or 23 years of age. According to what Maeda heard, they were told, "You can be companions to Harriman's son and if you like, you can attend school." However kind that oral promise may have been, in the end the youths were sent back to Japan. [64]

---

[64] Cartoon showing Edward Harriman (1848~1909.) He was suspected of trying to build a monopoly.

第十一勝 *Daiju-chisho*
Eleventh Victory
Shikago Ensei
Travelling to a Duel in Chicago

Chicago, Illinois circa 1900

Mr. Harriman had returned from his trip to Japan just as the Portsmouth accord was being signed. Maeda supposed as a souvenir of his trip to Japan he thought he might bring over some living Japanese martial artists. On the other hand, just prior to this Mr. Hill had invited Yamashita Nanadan to be an instructor to his children. As it turned out his wife was opposed, and the situation changed. However, Mr. Hill used his connections to find Yamashita Nanadan a position at Harvard University and the Naval Academy. The newspapers also frequently reported on Hill's admiration of

Japanese Judo and if Yamashita Nanadan happened to be in the paper, you always saw Mr. Hill's name next to it. On the other hand, Harriman was the exact opposite of Hill. Mr. Harriman strutted proudly into Japan and on his return brought Japanese martial artists home as souvenirs. The way Mr. Harriman rid himself of these two martial artists was inconsolable. The Kendoka was Isoyama Ryunosuke and the Judoka was Kodokan Nidan Kaku Yoshihara, both of the Butokukai in Kyoto.

Around this time, there were about ten Judoka spread around New York, Boston and Washington DC. While not all of them were working professionally as Judo instructors, if they had a chance to teach or work as an assistant, they did. Meanwhile Maeda continued to work as a Judo instructor at the Dojo, waiting for another chance to travel to Europe. One day, a Japanese student who was studying abroad at Yale University stopped by the Dojo. He was collecting money for veterans of the Japanese-Russian war to send home, and he asked Maeda and company to participate in an event. So Maeda, along with the young Kendo practitioner Isoya and the Judoka Kaku Nidan agreed to participate in the fundraiser. On the day of the event, the students put on some sort of crude play that may have been a tragedy or may have been a comedy, it was hard to tell. After that Maeda and company did their demonstration. The auditorium at the school was filled so a great many people got to see Japanese Judo.

It was now the beginning of February of Meiji 39, 1906, so it was very cold, and snow was beginning to accumulate. Throughout February Maeda continued to teach at the New York Dojo, though it was hard going, and he was expecting this to continue into march and April. However, towards the end of the month, he received another invitation from the Chicago Athletic Club. The letter stated, "Our new building will be finished in the near future, and we would like to have a Judo instructor at the club. Would you be able to do a lecture and demonstration?" Maeda was a bit suspicious regarding the phrase, "Our new building will be finished in the near future..." however the club had included round-trip train fare as well as money for his accommodation and meals, so it seemed a reasonable offer.

Since, it seemed he would be living in Chicago for the foreseeable future, so it would mean giving up the name he had built for himself here in New York and starting over in Chicago. He would have to start from scratch building up his base. He should have thought about it a bit more, but since Maeda had already sent a reply stating that he accepted, he was committed to going. The club wanted him there for their spring event and though he thought something about this smelled fishy, he decided to be there by the appointed time.

So, at the spring exhibition Maeda and Tomita Rokudan did as before, demonstrating Kata and so on. The building was only one third complete and it wasn't going to be finished until the following spring. "Finished in the near future" indeed. However, since Maeda had left New York with the intention of becoming a Judo instructor for the Chicago Athletic Club, he couldn't well turn around and go back to New York.

As it turned out, at Chicago University there was a Japanese man who had accompanied Maeda and Tomita to Japan. He was high-level Shihan Yamanouchi Shigeo, who was working as an assistant professor of botany. So the two of them got together and arranged for a one-day Judo demonstration in the gymnasium, hoping it would lead to a club forming.

At this point Maeda was well acquainted with how these sorts of events went and he ended up facing off against of the strongest student-wrestlers at the school. Predictably he took on the first student "naked" meaning with no Keikogi, so the duel was American style, meaning the goal was to see who could press the other's shoulders to the mats first. However, this student was not particularly experienced and so Maeda used the technique that had worked for him down south, namely pushing his arms out to the side. This gave him a win without much effort. The next student dropped down on one knee in a guard defense. This duel turned out to be quite a struggle. Since Maeda was going to stay away from Gyaku and Shime because they were kind of rough, he was limited to throwing techniques. It was quite difficult, and Maeda was perplexed for a time, However, he was eventually able to get a good grip around the student's waist and raise him up before throwing him. Maeda landed on top of him and quickly got the pin. The exhibition had ended in success.

However, when talking to the students they said, "It is nearly summer vacation, so we would like to arrange for a class to start in the fall with the new semester." This was not exactly what Maeda was hoping for. A few days later he did a demonstration and lecture at an athletic university for girls. That school was also interested in a Judo program, but not until the new school year starting in the fall. It was around this time that a certain story in the paper about a young woman who used Judo to disable a giant male attacker ran in the paper. Since the story also contained an illustration of the girl, many girls became extremely interested in Judo. Be that as it may, when it came time to actually do training, most found other things to do and the plan fell by the wayside.

ボストンの涼風 *Boston no Ryokaze*
The Fine Breeze in Boston

Washington Street in Boston, 1906.
Image courtesy of the Library of Congress

Maeda and company tried at various athletic organizations, but it was to no avail. They even reached out to a Girls Athletic School however they never received a clear answer and soon gave up. As this continued it became summer. Winters in Chicago were colder than in New York and in the spring the wind off Lake Michigan cut like a knife. However, when summer rolled around, it was so hot it felt like you were frying. While up until now Maeda had only worried about enduring the cold, now with the advent of summer it was so humid it threatened to be the death of him, and he was miserable. He had tried everything he could think of to find a position in Chicago, but it wasn't meant to be. Ever since he had arrived in America, New York had served as his home base and, as the saying goes, "An old river never runs out of water." He thought seriously of returning to New York.

Around this time Tomita Rokudan was trying to recruit two female assistant instructors. He ran an ad in the paper and, in a demonstration of how interested Americans were in the subject of Judo, got around a dozen replies. From amongst them he chose two girls who were young and had strong bodies from doing gymnastics training. So, Tomita Rokudan taught them the Taiso no Kata. Then, he and his assistants went to a city just outside of Chicago called Milwaukee which was quite famous for its brewery. Tomita and his two beautiful assistants gave lessons in Taiso no Kata every day for a week at a local theater. Maeda was there to help Tomita demonstrate Kata. Later, Maeda did Randori with the largest men in attendance. The whole demonstration was very well received and there was a large crowd every night.

While Maeda and company thought that was the best way to introduce Judo, many Japanese living the US probably thought they were making it into a form of entertainment. When they had arrived in America, Maeda and company had sought to present Judo as it would have been presented in their own society, thus presenting Judo as they were now in Chicago would have been seen as crass. However, they were now realizing with regret that this sort of big event is what they should have done from the beginning. After arriving they never seemed to be able to demonstrate Judo as they wanted to and unfortunately, that was at the time when interest in Judo was spreading like wildfire. Now they had the sense that interest in Judo was waning. As if on cue, the weather, which was becoming hotter, made indoor sports intolerable and Maeda and company ended the show after a week.

However, just as this show was wrapping up a man from Chicago came to them with an offer. This summer he was planning to form a class in Springfield, the hot springs resort, and wanted to recruit a teacher. They were stunned by the offer, which came just as they were feeling quite miserable at their state of affairs, as if a dark cloud were hanging over them, truly fate moves in mysterious ways. They immediately agreed to the plan however there was a wrinkle. The man offering the job would not pay the room and board of two people. Maeda's thinking on the matter was, "Now we are subsisting on breadcrumbs pinched off a big loaf, so if he agrees to our salary demands, that would be grand. However, if not, and we have to move away from Chicago, not towards New York, but towards San Francisco, we could well end up in trouble if we try and say "Hey! This isn't what we agreed to! How are we supposed to get back to New York?"

Despite Maeda's appeal, the man would not alter the conditions of the contract, so he relented. Though Maeda had planned on continuing with Tomita Rokudan, a man he had great respect for, after consulting together they agreed to separate. Tomita Rokudan would accept the contract with the man from Chicago and teach Judo in Springfield. Tomita went to Springfield and found the man from Chicago had hired an assistant for him under a separate contract. Later, Maeda heard that the man was a "Mountain Priest," or con artist, who didn't fulfill the contract he had signed. This resulted in him being taken to court. Japanese residing in the area did all they could to help Tomita Rokudan win his court case. Despite winning, Tomita was unable to receive full payment of his wages and had a lot of trouble.

In June, while Tomita was in Springfield, Maeda returned to New York. That year, in Revere Beach, a popular summer getaway near Boston, a new Japanese village had set up. The day after Maeda returned to New York, the manager of the village presented himself and asked if Maeda would be interested in starting a Judo class at the village. While riding the steam locomotive to New York, Maeda though about what his next move would be, considering he hadn't really hit on a viable plan so far. He recalled how he had missed his chance to travel to Europe and disembarked from the train feeling disheartened. However, in a stroke of luck he had a job offer at Revere beach and this rejuvenated Maeda, who was now overjoyed. This time alternated between hits and misses and it made Maeda feel as if he were a blind gambler wandering about.

Thus, it came to pass that Maeda linked up with Kaku Nidan and went to the Japanese village. The village had been having problems finding a real teacher as "Mountain Priests," or charlatans, seemed to abound. However, the pair presented themselves properly. These were their countrymen after all. The contract was carefully negotiated, and the salary was deemed appropriate, so they eventually held their first demonstration and training. So, they had finally found a solution to their problem of where to find bread, which had worried them since they left Chicago. Maeda would never forget the clean taste of the beer he drank that night while feeling the cool ocean breeze on the observation deck.

Maeda Mitsuyo (center) in Boston around 1906
© The Kodokan Institute

A JUDO WARRIOR'S JOURNEY AROUND THE GLOBE・世界横行柔道武者修業

第十二勝
Daijunisho
ビール樽腹の大男 *Biru Taru Hara no O-Otoko*
The man with a belly like a beer barrel

Japanese Village, Revere Beach 1907

At last, with his job at the summer resort at Revere Beach, Maeda could breathe a sigh of relief. Every morning he trained with several members of the Dojo. The afternoon was spent mostly doing classes open to the public. In case someone was interested in dueling him, Maeda put a notice out front saying that he would accept any challenge. However, despite being there for a month, no one challenged him. One day, a man did appear and challenged Maeda. He easily weighed over 30 Kan, 113 kilograms. If compared to a contemporary Sumo wrestler, he was bigger than either 133-kilogram Kunimi or 150-kilogram Tachiyama. He wore a smirk on his face and seemed to be quite strong. Since Maeda had been twiddling his thumbs since he arrived at the Japanese village, even if a demon presented himself Maeda wouldn't have refused the duel. Maeda quickly agreed and the date of the duel was set.

The big man looked down on Maeda and had clearly decided he would crush the Japanese man in one squeeze of his fist, so he agreed to wear a Keikogi and donned it without comment. The rules were settled as well and included both Gyaku and Shime. Throws would only count as a victory if both shoulders touched the ground. This man was extremely fat, and his belly extended so far it was like it was a barrel of beer. Since his face was flushed and he had a double chin Maeda wondered if he would even be able to move. As he watched the man, his hands moved with surprising quickness. However, it was clear the man had no experience dueling with a Judoka since he did not drop his hips and edge forward looking to apply a stratagem. Instead, he simply charged forward like a wild boar. Even for a Judoka dealing with a 30 Kan man charging at you can be difficult, especially if you only weigh 18 Kan. One mistake will mean getting knocked down and then pinned.

This was an important match and Maeda had girded his loins. If he was still in the curious southern area of the US, and was defeated by an injury, it would not have any great bearing on his future. However, since he had made his Dojo here, in the Japanese village at the beach near Boston and was surrounded by his fellow countrymen, if he made a mistake and lost this duel, his prestige would be affected. Since he was only just now beginning to eat good bread again this was an important duel indeed. His plan was to avoid his opponent's initial attacks. The man came at him two or three times and Maeda managed to stay clear of his opponent's arms, which were like iron, however he nearly stumbled from his own inertia. At any rate, simply grabbing hold of Maeda wasn't going to lead to his victory. If Maeda could keep him from wrapping those great arms around his back, he would be fine. His attacker seemed to be content to chase Maeda all over the mats. While Maeda's fellow countrymen watched the match with apprehension, the American spectators were having a fine time of it. They shouted their support of the American man and made queer noises and whistled. Clearly, they were under the impression that Maeda was about to be cornered.

Up until now Maeda had deftly avoided his opponent's attacks, like he was walking along the edge of a sword blade. At this point, Maeda was standing on the spot where his opponent had stood when they started the match. From his opponent's perspective, Maeda had only sought to escape the whole time, so he responded by spreading his long arms wide, like he was trying to catch a person in a game of tag. Maeda allowed a grin to spread on his face. Grabbing the giant man's right he planted his leg in front of the giant's right knee and then pulled the man down with Hiza Guruma. The 113-kilogram man crashed to the ground hard enough for the vibration to be felt. The sight of the giant going down was quite comical and the Japanese in attendance guffawed loudly and their cheers showed no signs of flagging.

The giant was angry, and he scrambled to his feet, face red. He charged in and grabbed Maeda's lapels like he was a beggar. This situation couldn't have been more perfect. Maeda slipped his right hand in and moved in deep, setting his hips before throwing with a huge Koshi Nage. The giant's feet went up towards the ceiling and he crashed down on his head. This throw seemed to have rattled the giant because when he came again, his hips were lowered, and he aimed for Maeda's legs. Maeda grabbed both sleeves and yanked him forward. The moment the giant resisted by pulling back, he rose and Maeda used this chance to pull him around in a half-circle. It was a curious sight; Maeda was yanking him around like a toy or like an ant trying to carry a grain of rice.

The giant realized he was being toyed with and that it was making him look foolish, so he resisted with all his might, rising up. In that moment Maeda attacked with Tomoe Nage which threw the giant man in a huge arc overhead. The man had never seen anything like this unexpected attack and with his arms and legs rigid in surprise went tumbling to the ground. Maeda stayed with him and pushed his sleeves out to the sides and, ignoring the giant's wild resistance, got the pin.

For the next round Maeda seized the giant's sleeves right as the round began and gave the giant a sample of Tsurikomi Goshi, his specialty. As the giant was scrambling to rise, he followed up by toppling the man with Okuri Ashi Barai. Like a man in his death throes, he snatched Maeda's left leg as he fell. He yanked hard and Maeda, getting pulled in an unexpected way fell onto his butt. However, Maeda was able to get the giant's right arm in between his thighs. He went for a Gyaku, joint lock, however the giant seemed to have no idea what was going on, because he proceeded to try and violently escape. Suddenly in the midst of his floundering he gave out a strange cry of *Ah!* Maeda too had felt something and released his grip with a sigh of relief of *Hah!* The giant was sitting on the ground feeling sorry for himself and when Maeda looked at the giant's arm, it was clear his elbow had been dislocated. The Americans in attendance were in an uproar. They stood up and began booing, and the Japanese in the audience followed their lead and stood up as well. The giant, who had been sure of his easy kill was now crying out "I give, I give!" With that the referee announced, "We have a winner!"

The dislocated joint was soon fixed, and the uproar didn't last much past that. Maeda had won a total victory. He felt he had won an important bout even though his opponent had been something of a blockhead.

A JUDO WARRIOR'S JOURNEY AROUND THE GLOBE・世界横行柔道武者修業

慕斯頓魔窟の夜嵐
A Stormy Night in Boston's Rouge's Alley

The train shed and yard in Lynn, Massachusetts for the locomotive running from Revere Beach to Boston.

After Maeda had made the giant wallow in his own misery no one else came to challenge him, so he passed the days teaching Judo. Someone suggested a Gekken, Japanese fencing, demonstration. Since Maeda was well versed in Gekken training, he was proficient enough for a beginner's class. [65] So, with a feeling of nostalgia for the days he used to train this martial art, he donned his Men, helmet, and Kote, hand and wrist guards. Maeda's partner in this sword fighting demonstration was a man named Sata, who was a painter. For Americans, who had never seen such a display, the two were more than qualified.

An acquaintance of Maeda from Waseda University, Koyama Tanizo, who was attending Harvard University, also arrived to assist. Koyama and Maeda were at Waseda at around the same time and frequently saw each other at the Waseda Dojo. The man's style was

---

[65] 撃剣 Gekken, also read as Gekiken, was a pre-Kendo form of dueling that included body-checks and take-downs. Generally speaking, duelists were allowed to trip or grab the other opponent.

quite dramatic, and he shouted grandly as he took Daijodan, upper stance, much to the delight of the audience. In addition, another acquaintance, Nakagawa Suekichi who was studying abroad at Yale University, happened to be sightseeing at the summer getaway and decided to lend a hand. This group, along with several American students, Fukano Eiji from Waseda University and several local Japanese trained every morning in the intense summer heat. In the afternoon they went fishing and generally passed the summer enjoyably.[66]

One night Maeda and a friend decided to go to Boston in the evening so they could see the skyline at night. The locomotive took less than two hours to get there, so around the time the evening breezes were picking up and the windows of the beach houses were beginning to be shuttered, they set out from Revere beach.[67] Upon arriving in Boston, they could see the fronts of not only 5 and 6 story

---

66
- Koyama Tanizo 小山谷蔵 (1876 ~ 1951) Became a government official working for the Ministry of Foreign affairs.
- Nakagawa Suekichi 中川末吉 (1874 ~ 1959) Became president of Furukawa Electric and later Nippon Light Metal Inc.
- Fukano Eiji 深野英治 (unknown)

67

Map of the train line connecting Revere Beach to Boston

buildings but ones of 12 or more, like giant soldiers standing abreast. The buildings completely blocked the wind so it was like walking in a cauldron.

It was quite extraordinary; the gas and electric lights illuminated the beautiful decorations in front of the shops. Casually dressed gentlemen and ladies walked together not looking at anything in particular and chatted. They moved in and out and past each other like a piece of weaving. Amongst them, "white-necks[68]", who sometimes dressed like high-class women, sometimes dressed like pure girls from good houses, were seeking prey by called out "Over here! Over here!" Maeda and his companion were able to resist their sultry gazes which were like a cormorant or a hawk hunting its prey.[69]

Light was pouring out of the windows of the cafes and bars and inside they were packed with customers enjoying the long summer nights. Seeing these sights for the first time Maeda exclaimed, "From time to time the sights, sounds and smells of this kind of place can be exhilarating." They stopped in a restaurant for a cold beer and enjoyed the cool taste of ice cream from another. Now they were exhausted.

Maeda and his companion were blissfully carefree in both body and mind, as they ambled about uninhibited, as freely as winter winds, observing the sights and sounds. At around 10 pm, Maeda's friend departed, and Maeda began thinking it was time to head home. Looking at a clock he realized the train would soon depart. "If I am late, I'm liable to be thrown in the heavy penalty house.'" Maeda was worried if he missed the last train he would be stuck paying for a cheap flop house for the night. Since he was in a hurry he went to the horse-drawn carriage stand.

"Oi! I need to get to the train station that will take me to the beach! I'm in a hurry!" "You got it!" the driver replied, and he swung his long whip like a wave, cracking it one time and they started off. The driver drove expertly through the crowd and built

---

[68] *Shirokubi* 白首 "White-necks" referred to the make-up applied to the necks of low-class prostitutes.

[69] *Unome Takanome* 鵜の目鷹の目 Watching for prey as carefully as a cormorant or a hawk.

up a good head of speed. It was night and Maeda was in an unfamiliar town and unsurprisingly Maeda had no idea where he was. However, he had told the man to go to the train station and he had immediately replied in the affirmative, so Maeda was feeling quite full of himself. "Clearly, I have gotten a lot better at English recently!" Maeda was sitting in the back of the carriage enjoying his buzz from the alcohol as the driver was encouraging his horses. He was turning left and right down various streets and it was all looking the same, until they came to a place that looked like the outskirts of town.

Maeda looked about and, it seemed to him, that this was a different direction from the station where he had disembarked earlier in the evening. This didn't look like the road leading up to the station he had used either. "Hey, something is wrong!" he said as he began to feel the first tingling that something was awry. However, Boston was a big city, there may well be three or four stations that have trains heading for the beach. The driver said he understood, so he was perhaps heading to the one he knew best and Maeda decided to leave it up to the running hooves of the horses.

Around the time Maeda judged they had travelled for 30 minutes at a good clip, they arrived at a crossroads and the horse-drawn carriage turned down a narrow street. The place seemed like the sort to be populated with thieves and Maeda felt a tightness in his chest as if he were about to be attacked. He thought about calling out to the driver but since the horses were running at a full gallop the carriage was flying down the road. It seemed he was acting too late. Maeda raised himself up in his seat and looked forward. Suddenly it was very bright in front of him, the horse-drawn carriage had again turned on to a wide avenue and on either side were of curious design, and not at all like the city streets he had been walking earlier in the evening. While there were a few scattered light posts that lit parts well, the rest of the area was very dim.

Maeda moved up close to where the driver sat. "Hey! This is right? Is there a station near here?" Looking around Maeda could see nothing that resembled a train station. Suddenly the carriage, which had been racing along furiously, came to a sudden stop in front of a big building that looked like a hotel. "Here we are!" the man replied curiously as Maeda felt a sense of foreboding. Summoning all the power he could he demanded firmly,

"Hey, is this the station?" The driver turned around and showed his teeth, "Yup!" he said jovially. Looking at Maeda with a predatory gaze he said, "What are you on about? This is where you said you wanted to go?"

"I told you that I wanted to go to a train station so I could get to the beach, and you said that you understood!"

The man's eyes gleamed, "The train station? Surely you must be joking my friend, from here you can take the train straight to heaven! Angelic women await you! Stop talking crazy and pay me three dollars! ($98) That's a bargain for leading you to heaven! There is a stunningly beautiful woman waiting to tumble around in the sheets naked with you! As for me I am awfully late getting home, and I need to have a drink before I go to bed." Maeda realized he had been set up. He had been enjoying himself walking around town and when he finally realized he was running late for the train, he got ensnared by this man and was now in a tight spot. He briefly considered gamely paying the man...but three dollars was expensive, and an outrageous request. "I asked you to take me to the station and you tricked me and now I have missed the train. I intend to pay you however three dollars is not acceptable. Here, use this for your drink!" and he put a dollar (33$) into the man's hand.

The driver's face twisted, and he glared at Maeda with eyes that seemed to have turned white in their fury, and he clucked at Maeda "Don't try some joke on me, look how late it is! Who is out at this time of night thinking they can pay a dollar for a ride? Hell, three dollars is cheap! Don't try and talk me down, hurry up and pay me my three dollars! It's a bargain and I'm done for the night and want to hurry up and get home! Come on! Pay up!"

The driver was talking to Maeda in the most contemptable fashion. Maeda finally concluded, "No doubt because he realized I was a stranger to Boston, his guy was, from the very beginning, planning to drag me to this section of town by force and then demand an exorbitant fee." Thinking this he became more and more irritated, and he started grinding his teeth and unconsciously flexing his fists. But when he stopped to think about it, he realized that if he walked away from this horse-drawn carriage, he would have no idea which direction to go. He was like a lost child not knowing which direction was east and which was west. "I do not wish to exacerbate this situation, I will pay you the three dollars that you asked,

Maeda had missed his train and would have to stay at a hotel and then get a carriage to the station tomorrow, all told this would easily cost him three or four dollars. Calculating the cost in his head made him depressed, but he had been able to control his anger and offered a compromise to the driver. However, the driver was now ready to show his true colors and he suddenly became intensely angry shouting, "You cheap bastard, stop complaining and pay me three dollars!" as he climbed down from the driver's seat. He rapidly advanced on Maeda shouting in a lowly manner, "Listen you, if you don't want to pay then I will have to twist your arm and make you!"

The situation had changed rapidly and there was no one to complain to so Maeda opened the door and leapt down from the carriage before he got trapped inside. Taking a step towards the driver he glared at him and said, "Listen here you thug, don't think that you can fool me, I won't pay a single cent more of that illegal charge! Take your dollar and go home and be happy about it! I won't let you continue to threaten me, I will call a police officer!"

Maeda looked at the front of the hotel. It was far grander than the houses on either side, so he went up and knocked on the big front door. Fortunately, the door opened almost immediately. Maeda surmised that this whole area was part of Boston's red-light district and the house he stood before was some sort of hotel or tearoom. Maeda was planning to slip right inside the hotel but the carriage driver, who was running up behind Maeda, shouted out some sort of code-word to the doorman.

The doorman, who up until now had been ready to let Maeda pass suddenly blocked his path and shouted, "Get out of here!" Maeda retorted, "This is a hotel, isn't it?!" The man spat, "What are you barking about? A hotel?! Do you think we are going to let a dirty Chinese man in here?!" With that the giant doorman grabbed Maeda by the lapels and started shoving him out the door.

Maeda fired back, "What are you talking about you idiot?! I am not Chinese, I am of the country that recently won the war, Japan! If you keep being rude, I will make sure you regret it." Though Maeda spoke fiercely, it was to no avail. The doorman at the brothel shouted back, "What do you mean being rude? You are nothing more than an uppity Jap!" He was a big man, and he used all his strength to grab Maeda by the collar and shove him back. "Don't you know? This is the most famous brothel in Boston! You idiot!" And from behind he kicked Maeda in the butt.

It wasn't much of a kick, and he wasn't injured but Maeda had been attacked by an enemy and he was beyond being able to handle this situation calmly. He became a raging fire and completely forgot where he was and what he was doing. With a head full of rage, he grabbed the giant doorman/pimp's left collar with his right hand and, as he hoisted the man up in the air, he swung his left leg forward hard enough to break a bone and swept the man's legs out from under him. The attack took the pimp completely by surprise and he barely had time to shout *Ah!* in surprise before he landed upside-down on the ground. In answer to the blow, he received earlier, Maeda kicked the man in the side with enough force that the man was sure to remember it for some time. He grunted an "Un!" And did not move any more. "What a weakling!" Maeda thought.

However, looking at the man he thought, "Maybe I overdid it, has he regained consciousness?" While he was occupied with this thought, that bastard driver had started to charge Maeda from the side, his eyes flashing with rage as he swung down with an iron fist. Maeda, who became aware of the man, used his left hand to sweep away his iron fist, dropped his hips as he drew right up against the man and threw him with Koshi Nage. Maeda had thrown with all his power and the man crashed down onto the paving stones that made up the road. He made a *Guh!* Sound but did not rise right away. In fact, he was incapable of rising however he shouted repeatedly in a loud voice, "Police! Police!"

Back when he was living in Tokyo, Maeda would often go to the area around Karuazaka or Tomizaka and get completely drunk and rowdy. Almost every night, no matter where he was, he was acting like a barbarian and throwing people hither and yon. Invariably one would call the police and since he hated being dragged to the station and given a dressing down so Maeda opted for the simplest of the 36 Stratagems, escape.[70] He had a mantra he

---

[70] *Sanjurokkei Nigeru ni Shikazu* 三十六計逃げるに如かず "Of the 36 Strategies, escape is best (in this case.) This famous quote is from *Heiho Sanjurokkei* 兵法三十六計 The *Thirty-Six*

told himself after he had thrown a man he had been arguing with, "Get out while the getting is good!" So he shot off in the dim light and ducked into an alley with absolutely no idea where he was going.

As he dashed down the alley, in a stroke of the worst possible luck he realized with a start that a huge police officer loomed before him like a towering thunderhead blocking his way. It was now too late to turn back and find another way. Maeda wasn't afraid of the police officer himself, however he absolutely did not want to be hauled to the police station. Tangling with a police officer was strictly off limits since the after-effects of such a fight could be quite severe. That being said, Maeda wanted desperately to put this place behind him. He moved back and forth, back and forth looking for an opening, but the officer suddenly seized his sleeve.

Holy smokes, to call this man a giant soldier would be a mistake but if you were to order a "extra-large police officer" this is what you would get. The man filled the entirety of the alley and he would have easily noticed any normal pedestrian but the moment he came running down the alley, the policeman fixated on Maeda, marking him as his target. In this narrow alley there was no way to avoid him and he was trapped like a rat. The officer was easily 3 or 4 Sun over 6 Shaku, 189~192 centimeters, and he strode purposefully towards Maeda, grabbing him like the talons of an eagle snatching its prey. His strength was truly something to behold.

Just then the carriage driver appeared, having finally recovered, shouting, "Officer! Officer! Don't let him get away!" The officer replied, "Relax, it is taken care of!" The officer pulled Maeda by the collar from the alley into the light of the main road. The driver scampered up and the officer addressed him in the manner particular to highly trained police, "This is the man who attacked you?" The driver replied shaking (nodding?), "Yes sir, yes indeed!"

Stratagems by the Tan Daoji 檀道濟 (? ~ 436.) The book was not widely known until a copy was discovered in China in 1941. After being positively reviewed by a Chinese Communist Party paper, the book became widely read and was taught in schools, becoming more well-known than the Art of War.

Maeda couldn't believe it. "This is a total farce, this fat bastard abducted me, called me a Chinaman, and then called me a Jap after driving me all over creation for an hour and a half. Then after arriving here, I was finally able to get away from this man, but he still brazenly pursued me. He can hardly complain about getting thrown onto the paving stones. I kicked the pimp that lived in that house back there, he stopped breathing back there...."

The policeman suddenly interjected, "Hey! That guy is dead?!" and he looked around at the pimp laid out on the ground. Without saying a word, he slapped Maeda across the side of his face.

For his part, Maeda expected the Policeman to turn to him and say, "Well, we had better head over to the station." or some such, so he was caught completely off guard. Not only did he have no chance to dodge the blow, but he was caught flat-footed, and the full brunt of the blow hit him, and now he was furious. This was not something a police officer should do. Maeda shouted at the officer with the fury of one who was ready to throw a man down hard enough to kill him, "What are you doing?! There is no forgiveness for an officer acting so illegally, I am going to kick you to death!"
While Maeda's words were big, the giant police officer was easily a head taller than him and Maeda had to lean back and glare up at the man from below. Not a very good position to intimidate someone from. A great leering smile split the face of the officer, who loomed as large as Mt. Hitachi and he laughed derisively, "You little impudent man, you are going to get what's coming to you!" With that he threw a punch at Maeda.

From the way he punched Maeda figured the officer had done some boxing however it didn't matter if it was boxing or saber fighting, Maeda was in a fury and saw nothing but a foolish man. Using his left hand, he first deflected the officer's punch then snatched hold of that arm. Dropping down and pressing his body up against the man he gave the officer a taste of Seoi Nage. His body was thrown upside down and his hips struck the paving stones hard with a Boom! He scrambled to get up but couldn't quite manage from the pain. Instead, he sort of crawled about like a cat, wobbling the whole time. Meanwhile the carriage driver was running around in circles, howling in panic.

Maeda, having completed a grand technique, prepared to make good his escape but the officer, like a cornered fox farting in the face of its pursuer in a desperate final gambit, began blowing on his whistle with a *Byu-Byu!* sound.[71] The unbelievably shrill sound pierced the night and no doubt could be heard across half the city. Soon the sound of running feet could be heard and in a sudden burst of activity, men burst from every direction, converging on the scene. There were two more policemen and two or three giant firefighters. "Stop you bastard!" they shouted surrounding Maeda and blocking his escape. Maeda was back out on the well-lit main road with a chattering crowd forming. In front of him he had five giant opponents, shouting for him to stop in the name of the law. Then one threw a boxing style punch.

Maeda was in trouble; he was surrounded on four sides with not so much as a Suntetsu[72] to his name. He ducked the swing a firefighter threw at him and the man struck only air. Maeda scrambled and somehow managed to grab the man and, using his power, threw him with a Yoko Sutemi, sending the firefighter tumbling like a ball. Maeda thought he could use that chance to get some distance but though the firefighter tumbled across the ground he recovered as nimbly as a monkey and immediately charged directly at Maeda's chest. Another police officer drew the 2 Shaku, 60-centimeter, baton at his side, and swung with such force it was clear he was hoping to shatter Maeda's bones to dust.

Even in the middle of the day, facing off against an opponent armed with a cudgel would be tough and now he was on a dimly lit street in the rough side of town. He blew out a breath *Ha!* and shifted his body to the left and raised his left arm to protect his head as he dropped his hips low. The policeman tried to track Maeda with his swing, relying on his strength, but the move had caused his blow to only strike air. This caused him to stumble into Maeda who scooped

---

[71] *Kitsune no Saigoppei* 狐の最後っ屁 "Last fart of the fox" referring to any method of last resort.
[72] *Suntetsu* 寸鉄 A type of concealed weapon. A rod of metal with a loop for your finger. The illustration below shows several Edo-era designs.

his legs up and threw him to the ground. They fell entangled, and Maeda followed up by slamming his knee into the policeman's side. The man let out a grunt of *Unnn!* and showed no signs of rising.

Maeda used the next moment to leap to the side like a bird taking flight and put his back to a nearby telephone pole. Now he wouldn't have to worry about someone striking him from behind. Before he could breathe out in relief at finding a small respite, the other policeman began directing the firefighters and all four attacked from the front. This fight was turning into utter chaos with five men all swinging at the same time. If they had been unarmed, Maeda felt sure he would have had a grand time throwing them down hither and yon like Shogi chess pieces however that cudgel the policeman wielded was frightening. If he made one mistake and caught a blow from that, powered by the strength of that giant man, it would be over and he most certainly did not want to die a dog's death in Boston's red-light district. What he needed to do is avoid getting too close and find some deft strategy to manipulate these four men, however his attackers were closing in relentlessly, and he had no time to conjure up an inner secret of martial arts. Thus, in a scene that you would see as part of an action sequence in a play, even more dramatic than something out of a novel, Maeda shouted "Ya! Ya! Ya!" as loud as he could which, surprisingly stopped all four men and they neither punched nor struck with a weapon.

In the corridor of a certain establishment in Yoshiwara, the red-light district in Tokyo, Maeda had brawled with a big group of construction workers. He had wrapped his left leg around the leg of the first man and pushed him in the chest with his right, toppling first him, then all the others like Shogi chess pieces. While he was quite proud of dealing with those workers so decisively, considering the situation he was in now, scrambling to stay out of the reach of four giant men, he needed to come up with a plan. He briefly considered charging straight at the group however, that would only serve to blunt their initial attack. They had seen the police officer Maeda had thrown laid out on the ground and were prepared and maybe even nervous. Well, realizing he had no choice other than attack them, Maeda became the angry tiger backed into a tiny recess, meaning all his ferocity was directed forward. He darted forward and with a *Ya!* set his foot and kicked the man to his right in the groin. If he had been the only opponent, Maeda would have used his hands, but he wouldn't have been able to deal with his second opponent if he was gripping the first man's body, therefore he went with a kick. His strategy was to keep his hands as a reserve unit. Maeda didn't get a very good strike on the man's groin but his knee had enough power in it to get his attention and he grunted *Ah!* and fell away. Upon seeing this, his next three opponents became cautious and took a step back out of Maeda's reach.

"Keep going!" Maeda thought, and he kicked the same man again, advancing. The enemy formation had broken up and was in disarray, but now they were trying to box him in again. Maeda realized he couldn't hesitate. The man he had kicked twice had lost a lot of his vim and vigor meaning that Maeda could afford to ignore him for the time being. Turning to face his other opponents, Maeda began kicking at them every way he knew how. These were pretty sloppy, amateur attacks due to Maeda's lack of training in that regard, however he seemed to land quite a few strikes on their legs. His attackers unconsciously recoiled from his disconcerting kicks. If you are stepping back when fighting, then you have already lost. The one who takes a step forward will advance ten paces towards victory. Maeda, realizing that the men were unlikely to respond in kind by charging him, he shouted as loud as he could and charged right through the middle of the men, kicking until he burst out past them.

Having made use of the opportunity to break through the men surrounding him, Maeda ran off in a straight line away from his attackers. He hadn't killed a person and hadn't robbed anyone so why would they care if a man they were fighting with ran off? At last, it seemed Maeda had made a smooth escape so he poured on the speed. However, he hadn't gone more than 5~6 Ken, 9~11 meters, before someone shouted, "Stop!" with great intensity. Maeda thought it might have sounded like one of the police officers, so he momentarily debated what to do. However, thinking, "If I stop, they are going to catch me." So, since no one blocked his path, he continued forward at a frantic pace, running 3 or 4 Ken, 5~7 meters, before he heard a "Boom!" that seemed to shake the earth and made Maeda's heart leap. "A pistol!" he realized. Checking his body, it didn't seem as if he had been hit though he hadn't stopped running. Then "Boom!" another shot rang out so loud it threatened to split the night apart.

Maeda's legs became weak and would no longer respond, "I don't want to get beaten to death like a dog..." he thought. The pimp who had been knocked out was certainly not dead and he had only thrown the first policeman as payback for that slap. "I haven't committed any crime!" he thought and finally realized, "If I keep going on like this I am going to get shot by that pistol!" So he stopped and turned around. The man approaching him appeared to be wearing a police officer's uniform. The man grabbed hold of Maeda's sleeve and he thought, "Now he's probably going to whack me with his cudgel..." and stayed on his guard. However, the man that had taken hold of his sleeve did not seem at all violent and, in fact, seemed quite calm. His uniform was neat and though he spoke with authority there was nothing untoward in his manner as he explained, "There is no need for you to escape, please accompany me to the police station. Our police department will not harm you, just come with me and tell us everything."

Maeda was somewhat mollified by this man, this police officer, and the calm respectful manner he used when interacting. Seeing his enemies behind him, Maeda realized to his chagrin, that his short legs were incapable of outdistancing these men. All this trouble started because he had tussled with that first police officer. He had tried to flee but when the pistol had come onto the scene that had come to a quick end. So, it looked like going with the police officer was his only real option now, so he turned to the officer and spoke as politely as he could, "You have spoken to me fairly and since I would very much like an opportunity to explain myself. Therefore, I will follow where you lead."

Just then the other police officer as well as the firefighters came running up in a ragged line, looking pleased that Maeda had been apprehended. They all had something to say, "We finally got you! Quite a tricky fellow this one, kicking people and all!" "He's as quick as a monkey, but we've got him now! He's not getting away! Let's beat him to within an inch of his life, eh!" "I have to say this fella can do some mysterious stud (stuff?), look how small he is and he threw our fellow, the pimp, and knocked him out. We can't take any chances with him, lets tie him up!"

As they went on and on disparaging Maeda, he became guarded and dropped his hips while angling his body perpendicular to the gathered men. Maeda thought, "Now that I've been captured it seemed they were going to do the equivalent of tie me in a sack and beat me....Well, that may be but if I'm going to die, I'm going to go down like a wild man, and the first one I'm going to attack is this police officer." With that, he began edging towards the man.

However, the police officer stepped forward and glared at the men and said authoritatively, "Shut up all of you! I've heard enough of your grumbling! This man has already agreed to go to the police station, if you all have a problem with that, you can come to the station as well!" Having been scolded the men turned and left, muttering all the while.

The officer then asked Maeda to describe what happened as he guided them to the police station. Maeda told the story in detail from the beginning, and since the officer listened keenly and said "I see, I see" from time to time, Maeda began to relax and feel he was out of danger. Suddenly, just as they reached the end of the next block something struck Maeda in the eye and he saw stars. He let out a groan of *Ahh!* as he realized someone had just punched him. The bastard that hit him was turning to run away, but Maeda grabbed him and was in the process of setting up to throw the sneaky bastard down hard enough to pulverize his bones, when the police officer shouted, "W-Wait!" and used his strength to stop the attacker. It turns out the man who had snuck up and struck Maeda was the firefighter Maeda had thrown earlier who was back seeking revenge. Maeda's eye hurt and was throbbing with a Doki-doki feeling of something twitching. The police officer had responded immediately, and the man was certainly intense however, this officer's straightforward manner of dealing with people caused Maeda to leave the matter to him.

Amazingly the police officer remained completely unruffled and calm, "Listen, this is the end of it, you will not have to endure anymore of this mischief. I think you are trustworthy, and I believe your story. Try and calm down and please think about what happened from beginning to end. From what I saw it seemed you were going to put a hurting on that man, and that is not something I can overlook as it is my duty to stop such things. It seems clear you gave those fellows a good beating so one punch is not such a bad price to pay, though I can't, in good conscience, condone such violence."

Hearing this reasoned explanation of the situation and the officer's responsibility Maeda was somewhat mollified, though he was still regretful that he had not been able to throw the sneak after grabbing him. Just thinking of breaking the man's fingers made the fingers of Maeda's hands flex and his palms go sweaty. However, the firefighter had slipped away like a cloud turning into mist. Later, upon reflection he realized that it was fortunate he hadn't broken the man's fingers.

The two continued towards the police station and the officer commented, "You know, earlier, if you had not of stopped running, I would have fired a third round, a real one, and I would have been aiming at you. I am always careful in such situations and would have aimed for your leg, so it would not have been a fatal wound, but there are no guarantees in such an intense situation, so it may have ended in a dangerous wound. It is possible to end up with a crippling injury that would last the rest of your life."

He continued, "Just to let you know, this is a rough area and it is not uncommon for murders and other violence to occur. As it gets late, there are a great number of customers wandering about, so it's up to us, police officers, to keep a watch on the whole area." So this area was one where the worst sort of violent thug could appear in front of you at any moment. Further, the carriage drivers and touts are all competing for customers and so every night there is no end to the threats, stealing of customers and reprisals. Maeda felt he had entered this domain like a blind snake. Now the barbarian-like manner of the pimp-doorman, the driver and even the police all fell into place. This was quite different from when he had tussled with the construction workers in Yoshiwara, where it was just two groups without any connection and his actions could be seen as a story to brag about. Here, Maeda realized, it was quite different, and he felt a bit ill.

So, the police officer eventually lead Maeda to the police station and he was questioned by the chief of police. First, he asked for Maeda's nationality, full name and so on and then asked him to describe the events that occurred. Maeda, for his part, did his best to explain what happened in English, however the captain only seemed to understand about half of what he said. Since the police officer that brought Maeda in was also able to explain what happened, the captain seemed to relax as the officer was able clarify the story. A foreign tourist had been first tricked then set upon by villains. The other patrolmen in the room listened with interest to the story and were clearly suppressing grins. Normally in such a situation when questioning someone about drunken brawl an officer would be saying something like, "What is this mess? You are in a heap of trouble..." however the situation was different, so Maeda was handled politely.

Thus, Maeda was in no way being questioned as a suspect since there was not a single hair of evil intent on his head. He had acted entirely in self-defense against his attackers. Unless the chief was planning on summoning the other parties involved and overseeing a resolution between all parties there was no reason to continue to hold Maeda at the police station. Unlike resolving a situation where both parties are from the same country, since two countries are involved, resolving the situation would require a lot of elaborate steps. The serious chief of the police station took all this into accounts and, smiling, faced Maeda and said, "Young man, you took a punch to the eye and that no doubt hurts, on the other hand I hear you threw those other fellows around something fierce in addition to kicking them. You knocked that pimp completely unconscious for a time, though now he has recovered. It seems everyone got hurt by the other so it's mutual combat. You also resisted being arrested by one of my officers and I cannot allow that to slide. I am going to fine you five dollars and send you home... however I am not going to collect the five dollars."[73] The captain's whole talk was more like a consultation than a policeman talking to a person he has detained.

The whole situation seemed like Maeda was talking something over with a friend. He laughed saying, "Wow, frankly I do not feel I have done anything bad enough to warrant a five dollar fine, however when looked at objectively this incident was quite melodramatic. I was expecting to remain as a guest in your facility and be placed in a dingy room for the night and then be brought before a judge in the morning. Clearly you spent more time on my situation that five dollars could hope to cover. As for me, I feel a little bit as if I was playing some part in an enjoyable game and therefore, I would like to offer five dollars to the police station.

---

[73] Equivalent to about $153 today.

While you may not think this is a great honor, I would like to offer it to show my approval of your deft handling of this situation." After stating the above in stumbling, awkward manner he finished by intentionally stringing together a few nonsense phrases, which made the whole group laugh.

So, Maeda was pulling out his wallet and readying to pay the five dollars before departing home when, laughing, the chief called him over, "You know you lost not only your coat but also your hat in that brawl earlier." Maeda went cold with realization. Initially he had taken off his coat and his hat must have flown off his head at some point in the scuffle and he hadn't even noticed. He had been standing in front of all these policemen talking as if he were a top-class gentleman. He couldn't suppress a grimace of embarrassment. It was summer so it was not out of the ordinary to walk around without a coat, but it was against the law to walk down the street without a hat. While it was a humorous situation, Maeda was also in a bit of a pinch. It was the middle of the night so all the shops would be shut. "I have no idea where I can buy a hat" Maeda thought, unconsciously rubbing his bare head.

"Where exactly are you staying?" the chief asked. When Maeda told him he was going to Revere Beach the chief looked around the room and finally pulled an old patrolman's hat out of a wardrobe. With a huge grin on his face he said, "Put this on before you go." "This was a very funny chief of police indeed" Maeda thought as he hesitantly placed the cap on his head and started to exit the office dressed curiously with no coat but wearing a patrolman's cap.

The chief called out to a large policeman standing to his side, "Hey, you! Take this man to a train station that will get him to Revere Beach!" The man replied, "Yes Sir!" but had a strange look on his face. Upon further inspection this was the police officer Maeda had tangled with earlier in the night and thrown, making him land hard on his hip. He had a big (bit?) of a mean looking smile on his face and said, "You are a pretty tough guy, you really put a hurting on me earlier. I can't understand how you could throw me, considering how small you are. I've never experienced anything like that in my life." He was looking at Maeda with wonder now.

"There is nothing mysterious at all about it. I am a Judo champion." Maeda said while looking around the room at everyone. "If you know Judo you don't need a stick or a pistol. Japanese policemen all practice Judo as part of their job, that is why they can capture criminals bare handed. Even if faced with an armed robber it is rare for a Japanese policeman to draw his saber[74] to subdue the criminal. Instead, they all use Judo to control the criminal as they tie him up." The chief nodded his head in understanding upon hearing this. He began expounding on Judo, "It is all clear now! I've always thought that art was mysterious. So you, young man, are the top Judoka of Japan! That's why you men all got beaten and bruised! I have no desire to go up against a Judoka!"

Once this topic was broached, all the policemen began talking about it. The chief went on to explain how he had seen Judo before, and the other men chimed in recalling newspaper articles they had read and so forth. Everyone's interest was piqued and Maeda, who had been preparing to leave, was suddenly thrust into the role of instructor. The chief of police wrapped his big arms around the Japanese man's chest and asked, "If you get grabbed like this, what do you do?" and "How do you tie up a criminal that is resisting?" So the police station suddenly became a Judo Dojo and Maeda began answering one question after another.

Since Maeda had long since missed his train, and it was looking like it wasn't long until morning, he got himself ready to train. He began his Judo lecture and demonstration for the whole police department. "No matter how you look at it, police officers should not be using their batons, because they lead to excess violence. To any person viewing the scene it seems murderous and is therefore not an appropriate way to handle a criminal in full view of the public, of which the police are the protectorate. Since the police rarely draw their sabers, the injuries incurred when arresting a criminal are few. In the era when police in Japan carried wooden poles, the people frequently viewed them with distrust, however in addition to Kendo the police also study Judo.

---

[74] Japanese police wore western-style sabers because Japan adopted many aspects of western policing after the Meiji Restoration in 1868.

Since they use this to subdue violent people bare-handed, serious injuries are rare.[75]

After giving this long-winded speech he looked at the police chief and his officers and realized they wanted actual training so he taught them two or three techniques that would be useful on the streets. The men were very interested and treated him with respect. So it seems the criminal had become a friend and had now become a Judo Sensei, directing his students in grand fashion. Eventually he made his farewells, and the patrolman took him to the train station and said good-bye.

Now, standing before the large building that was the train station and hearing the shrill blast of the steam whistle, Maeda thought, "Well that was certainly a curious night!" He laughed and began walking by himself towards the station. Though it was early in the morning, the newspaper boys were out and he passed groups of laborers, large and small. Those men, seeing Maeda wearing the old police officer's hat and without a coat, began whistling and hooting, "Look a Chinaman has turned into a police officer!" along with, "A cop must have gotten mugged and stripped of his possessions!" "Look Hakurai-Punch is here!" Gradually people began to gather around Maeda, and he did not care for how they gawked at him, so he dashed inside the station and got on the locomotive. He had played an interesting game last night and was planning on giving the hat to his friends as a souvenir when he got home. However, the crowd was still laughing and pointing at him and it was more than he could endure. Maeda traded the hat for a newspaper from a newspaper boy. In a letter back home Maeda

---

[75] The police department was established in 1874. Previously each domain in Japan had Samurai officials in charge of law and order. Initially, officers were armed with a Tebo, a 180 centimeter baton. However in 1883 the police were issued western-style sabers. In 1933 police carried a police-baton, a Tanto short knife and a handgun.

wrote, "Looks like I just missed out on bringing home an interesting souvenir."[76]

Upon returning to Revere Beach and regaling everyone with the story of his adventure of the previous night, his friends all shouted, "Why didn't you get a picture of yourself in front of the train station?!" as they held their bellies laughing. The following day the chief sent one of his detectives with a message asking if Maeda would teach Judo to the police. Having these somewhat unusual students join his Dojo was quite an endorsement of Maeda's skill. As it turned out the detective that brought him the request turned out to be a very dedicated student who devoted himself to training. After less than a month he was able to execute a great many techniques. Maeda would ask him "How did you go about restraining criminals yesterday?" and he would reply beaming, "Last night I was able to perfectly throw two violent louts!"

---

[76] The reference to Hakurai Punch is unclear. It perhaps relates to *Hakurai no Panchi* 舶来のパンチ refers to. It might be referring to the character on the cover of this Manga from 1909 titled *Hakurai Punch.* At any rate, some sort of insult.

Later Maeda's jacket, which had been left on the battlefield the other night was found and returned to him. It seems the detective had gone to great lengths to recover it. However, his hat could not be located. It no doubt died on the battlefield of the red-light district on the far end of Boston, probably as payment to the owner of that area. That night had been a savage, colorful and intense game.

Around this time a Japanese man who was studying abroad at Cornel University asked Maeda, "I received a request from a Japanese fellow I know in the UK. The letter asks if you would be interested in travelling to the UK and teach Judo?" The man went on to say that the contract would include travel expenses in addition to a reasonable salary. Clearly good things come to those that wait. At last, his long sought-after chance had come and he quickly agreed. The man said that the UK side would be sending a contract shortly.

Eventually September rolled around and the vacationers all went home. Maeda also decided to take his leave from the beach and he and Koyama Tanizo made their way to New York. While they were searching for an apartment they stayed in some hotel. One night upon returning to the hotel Koyama was putting his hand into his pocket and suddenly froze. He gave a small cry of "Ah!" Koyama had earlier received a transfer of $300 from Japan to pay for his Columbia University tuition, but he had fallen victim to a pickpocket. A lot of Japanese were under the impression that there weren't any pickpockets in foreign countries, however apparently this was a dangerous area for such thieves. Going after the money students carried in their pockets was cowardly indeed, but there was nothing to be done for it. Maeda had spent the summer at the beach in peaceful bliss but now he had been snapped back to reality, no doubt this portended ill fortune.

癒よ渡英の決心 *Iyo-iyo Toei no Kesshin*
At long last, the decision to go to the UK is made

Maeda could not endure another day at the hotel. As it turned out, a Ryokan, Japanese-style inn, had opened in New York and many Waseda University students were partial to it. The place was run by a chivalrous man named Ikuine Oh who previously worked for Okuma Shigenobu, the founder of Waseda University. Koyama commuted from the Ryokan to Columbia University and Maeda, as he usually did when he came back to New York, began teaching at the Dojo while waiting for the good news from London. As the 39th year of the Meiji Emperor, 1906, was ending the contract from London arrived. He signed and returned it and got himself ready so as soon as the travel money arrived, he would be ready to board a boat. However, the money to pay for his passage did not arrive.

Time passed and on January 1st of the 40th year of Meiji, 1907, Maeda celebrated his third New Year's in the United States. Since Mr. Ikuine had a restaurant attached to his restaurant (ryokan?) Maeda was able to enjoy traditional New Year's foods like Zonimochi, soup with vegetables and rice cakes, and drink Toso, spiced Sake. It was almost like he was back home in Japan. He and the other fellows staying at the Ryokan enjoyed their three-day holiday.

On the fifth of January two Frenchmen came by to pay him a visit, asking him to travel to Paris, "Our boat departs in two or three days, would you be interested in accompanying us? If you are agreeable, we can pay your travel expenses now. When have also brought a contract for you to sign. What do you say?"

Maeda couldn't believe his luck! It was turning out to be quite a fortuitous new year, however he told the men he couldn't answer right away, as he had already signed a contract to go to London. He told the men he would immediately dash off a telegram and would inform them of the response. The Frenchmen agreed and departed.

Maeda immediately sent a telegram to London and asked for a yes or no regarding the contract, however no response came no matter how long he waited. In his state of agitation, he could neither sit nor stand. "In all likelihood it has taken time for the telegram to get into the right hands." Maeda thought. Finally on the evening of the second day after he had sent his telegram, he got a reply. Opening it all that was written was "Wait." Did they think he was a fool? They were hanging him out to dry!

So, Maeda decided to give up on London and sent a message to the two Frenchmen asking them to come to his apartment the following morning at 9 or 10 am. However, though he waited until evening the next day, the two never appeared and their ship had departed. While he wasn't sure exactly what they were offering if he had taken the travel money, they had offered he would be on board a ship right now travelling to Europe. Maeda could not believe his ill fortune!

However, he was not completely disheartened as the telegram from London had said "Wait." Maeda was sure that a favorable reply would soon arrive bearing riches. He frequently sent letters inquiring as to the status of the contract and towards the tail end of January an envelope bearing documents arrived. "At last, my luck has changed, and good things are to come!" Maeda thought as he excitedly opened the envelope. However, as he opened the envelope that was addressed to him, he saw inside that there was a cancel of contract form. Maeda slumped down, dejected. This was outrageous! If the man who had made this offer was here now Maeda would have choked him to within an inch of his life.

He immediately contacted the Cornell University student who had acted as an intermediary and told him about how he was out of pocket all manner of expenses regarding his preparations to depart including telegrams and how he had lost a chance to go to France. He requested compensation for his expenses from the party in London. However, as the contract had been cancelled it seemed highly unlikely, they would respond.

For his part, the Cornell University student went to Maeda's lodging house and apologized profusely. With that Maeda's dream of going to Britain had come crashing down. All his efforts had been in vain, and it was hard to tamp down his indignation. However, Maeda suddenly decided this was simply one more challenge to overcome on his journey and though his goal was just out of reach, he would steadfastly take a step towards it. "I will simply pay my own passage across to Britain. By relying on other people, I have been disappointed, no matter what happens I will take a chance and cross over."

When he checked his wallet however, he did not have sufficient funds for passage. He couldn't but a first-class ticket and even a second-class ticket was out of reach. A third-class ticket would mean travelling like he was but one baby pig in a big litter, but considering the situation he was in, he had no other option. Having committed himself he made ready to go and purchase his ticket. Just as he was leaving however, Ikuine Oh, the owner of the lodging house, called out to him saying he wanted to talk with Maeda about something. Once in Mr. Ikuine's office, he said, "So at long last you are making your way over to London? That is a good plan, however I heard you are purchasing a third-class ticket? It is completely inappropriate for a Judo Sensei to be travelling third-class and would be remiss in allowing it. Here are some funds which I offer you as a parting gift as you begin your journey." With that he handed Maeda a paper envelope.

Maeda felt that mysterious events were occurring one after another and he was unable to see where fate would take him. His friends and acquaintances had each contributed a little and Maeda initially felt somewhat dishonest taking travel money from people he was friends with. Having accepted their help in covering his expenses he risked incurring ill-feelings if he failed. Maeda had made a difficult decision and prepared himself to depart as if doing a Sutemi, sacrifice throw, and it was this firm decision to act that had garnered Ikuine Oh's sympathy and his subsequent plan to organize offering assistance. Now Maeda was able to purchase a second-class ticket. The name of the boat was the *Cunard Line* and it was set to depart on the 2nd of February. From the night before departure snow had begun to fall and as he tried to walk out on the deck of the ship to wave farewell to his friends who had gathered to send him off, he was prevented by a great blizzard.

A Judo Warrior's Journey Around the Globe
America 1904 ~ 1907
End

MAEDA MITSUYO・前田光世

MAEDA MITSUYO・前田光世

Maeda in the News

As Reported in American Newspapers

Maeda's Journey in the News

The following are transcripts of newspaper articles from the time when was in America. The transcriptions are "as is" and sometimes the phrasing in these historical newspaper articles can be confusing.

None of the articles have been edited, rather they have been presented as is.

There are many interesting spellings of words such as Tokio (Tokyo) Jiu-do (Judo) and so on.

The Anaconda Standard
Friday January 13th 1905]

JAPAN'S MYSTERIOUS ART IN THE AMERICAN METROPOLIS

New York, Jan 12—"Oh, jiu-jitsu is a very simple matter when you once know the tricks. Here is this man. He comes at me as though to strike me. I pay no attention to his extended arm, with which he intends to guard himself, but I watch his other hand. As soon as he starts to strike I knock up his guard, so, catch his other arm and—"

There was a vision of a large human body flying through the air, describing circles in its flight, and the next moment a Japanese no larger than a good-sized American boy of 15 years was sitting on the chest of a 240-pound American. It was all done in a twinkling, and as the little fellow sat there he casually remarked, "That is the way I threw 'Ajax,' the policeman." "Tom" Sharkey, pugilist, was the victim.

Yatsuguma Higashi is one of the 70 sons of Japan who have received degrees for proficiency in the science of jiu-jitsu, which is pronounced "jewjit." Two others of these, Tomita and Yamashit, are in this country.

Impressed by the importance of the latest adopted method of defense, Police Commissioner McAdoo called Higashi to police headquaters, where he gave an exhibition of his skill, having several of the best known athletes and wrestlers of the force as his opponents. All went down before the Japanese with equal ease. He weighs only 115 pounds and stands 5 feet 3 inches in height. As he closed with each of the big men opposed to him he seemed a difficult task, but for a moment only. So successful was his exhibition that another will be given before the commissioner in a few days, after which it is probable that Hagashi will be employed to teach the art to New York policemen.

"The science is one of tricks," he said. "In Japan boys begin to study it in the grammar schools and continue it through their college courses. But only those who are known to be thoroughly good at heart are allowed to learn those tricks by which a man can be killed. So dangerous is the knowledge of the science to a man without good principles that we will not teach him.

"Every Japanese policeman is skilled at jiu-jitsu, and through it is not only able to attack a man, but to defend himself and give aid to the injured in the absence of a doctor. There are 160 movements in the science, and when a man knows all of them he is prepared for any emergency. I have heard jiu-jitsu called wrestling, but it is nothing of the kind. Wrestlers in Japan are not allowed to use it either by wrestling rules or by jiu-jitsu rules, and very few of them know anything about the science."

The Anaconda Standard
Friday January 13th 1905

Japan's mysterious art in the American metropolis

"Oh, Jiu-jitsu is a very simple matter when once you know the tricks. Here is this man. He comes at me as though to strike me. I pay no attention to his extended arm, with which he intends to guard himself, but I watch his other hand. As soon as he starts to strike, I knock up his guard, so, catch his other arm and—"

There was a vision of a large human body flying through the air, describing circles in its flight, and the next moment a Japanese no larger than a good-sized American boy of 15 years was sitting on the chest of a 240 pound American. It was all done in a twinkling, and as the little fellow sat there, he casually remarked, "That is the way I threw "Ajax" the policeman." "Tom" Sharkey, pugilist, was the victim.

Tatsugama Higashi.   *Ajax Whitman*

Tatsugama Higashi is one of the 20 sons of Japan who have received degrees for proficiency in the science of Jiu-jitsu, which is pronounced "jewjit." Two others of these, Tomita and Yamashita are in this country.

Throwing a 200LB Man Over His Back

Impressed by the importance of the latest adopted method of defense, police commissioner McAdoo called Higashi to police headquarters, where he gave an exhibition of his skill, having several of the best-known athletes and wrestlers of the force as his opponents. All went down before the Japanese with equal ease. He weighs only 115 pounds and stands 5 feet 3 inches in height.

As he closed with each of the big men opposed to him, his seemed a difficult task, but for a moment only. So successful was his exhibition that another will be given before the commissioner in a few days, after which it is probable that he will be employed to teach the art to New York policeman.

L : Breaking an Ordinary Strangle Hold
R : The Japanese Strangle Hold

"The science is one of the tricks." He said. "In Japan, boys began to study it in grammar school and continue it through their college courses. But only those who are known to be thoroughly good at heart are allowed to learn those tricks by which a man can be killed. So dangerous is the knowledge of this science to a man without good principles that we will not teach him."

New York Tribune
Friday February 3rd 1905

JIU JITSU AT HARLEM Y. M. C. A.

A jiu jitsu exhibition will be given at the Harlem branch of the Young Men's Christian Association this evening by Tsunejiro Tomita and Eisei Maeda. Tomita is prepared to meet all comers, and as a number of well known wrestlers are to be found in the membership of the association, several lively contests are expected.

Jiu Jitsu at Harlem YMCA

A jiu jitsu exhibition will be given at the Harlem branch of the young men's Christian association this evening by Tsunejiro Tomita and Eisei Maeda. Tomita is prepared to meet all comers and, as a number of well-known wrestlers are to be found in the membership of the association, several lively contests are expected.

Daily Utah State Journal
Wednesday February 22nd 1905

> Prof. T. Tornita and Y. Maeda of Tokio gave an exhibition of jiu-jitsu before 1,000 Princeton students yesterday. Prof. Tornita is said to have instructed President Roosevelt in the new manly art.
>
> Maeda called upon the students for volunteers to wrestle with him, and B. Tooker, the football player and champion wrestler, stepped forth. He was quickly thrown.
>
> Feagles, the gymnastic instructor, then took a turn. By a quick attack he put the Jap on his back, but the Princeton man soon lost the advantage and was easily downed.

Prof. T. Tomita and Y. Maeda of Tokio gave an exhibition of Jiu-jitsu before 1000 Princeton students yesterday. Professor Tomita is said to have instructed president Roosevelt in the new manly art. Maeda called upon the students for volunteers to wrestle him, and B. Tooker, the football player and champion wrestler, stepped forth. he was quickly thrown.

Feagles, the gymnastic instructor, then took a turn. By a quick attack he put the Jap on his back, but the Princeton man soon lost the advantage and was easily downed.

The Brooklyn Citizen
Wednesday March 22ⁿᵈ 1905

JEFF ON THE JIU JITSU.

His Press Agent Says Champion Will Endeavor to Teach K. Higashi a Few Things.

Samuel C. Mott, manager of James J. Jeffries, came to town at 2 o'clock yesterday afternoon and for the next two hours kept the wires hot between here and Greenville, S. C., getting the champion to express himself on the challenge of K. Higashi for a fight to a finish at jiu jitsu. Jeffries finally replied to Mott's telegrams as follows:

"Higashi? Who is he? Any relative of Tomita, whom the Military Academy boys downed at West Point? I have heard of these jiu jitsu fellows, but never knew of one who would not crawl when it came to the point on the issue of a coat hold, a vest or lapel hold, or the question of kicking and jumping on a fallen opponent. Say, does Higashi want me to meet him in my buckskins as Davy Crockett? I'll do it at that. No, I won't draw the color line on this Japanese nobleman. He can have my New York address when I come to town Saturday and meet me when and where he pleases. I forget, though—there are two challenges ahead of him, Adolph Zink and Arthur Dunn. Zink weighs seventy-five pounds and Arthur Dunn is in Higashi's own class, 115 pounds. When I've finished with 'em I'll wind up this Japanese midget, or if they like, fight all three in the same evening and finish up with Corbett and Fitzsimmons."

Jeffries will be in town from his Southern trip next Saturday or Sunday at the latest. He and Yank Kenney are planning a public exhibition of jiu jitsu for heavy weights in New York the week beginning April 3. They intend to show the superiority of the big fellows at this game, but if any Jap, small or big, cares to break into the game with them there is no doubt that he will be accommodated.

The Brooklyn Citizen
Wednesday March 22nd 1905

Jeff on the Jiu-jitsu.

This press agent says champion will endeavor to teach K. Higashi a few things

Samuel C. Mott, manager of James J. Jeffries, came to town at 2:00 o'clock yesterday afternoon and for the next two hours kept the wires hot between here and Greenville SC getting the champion to express himself on the challenge of K. Higashi for a fight to the finish at Jiu-jitsu. Jeffries finally replied to Mott's telegrams as follows:

"Higashi? Who is he? Any relative of Tomita, whom the Military Academy boys downed at West Point? I have heard of these Jiu-jitsu fellows, but never knew of one who would not crawl when it came to the point on the issue of a coat-hold, a vest or lapel-hold, or the question of kicking and jumping on a fallen opponent. Say, does he actually want me to meet him in my buckskins as Davy Crockett? I'll do it at that. No, I won't draw the color line on this Japanese nobleman. He can have my New York address when I come to town Saturday and meet me when and where he pleases. I forget though there are two challenges ahead of him. Adolf Zink and Arthur Dunn. Zinc weighs 75 pounds and Arthur Dunn is in Higashi's own class 115 pounds. When I finished with 'em I'll wind up this Japanese midget or if they like, fight all three the same evening and finish up with Corbett and Fitzsimmons."

The Brooklyn Daily Eagle
Wednesday March 22nd 1905

JIU-JITSU AT COLUMBIA.

Students Not Favorably Impressed With Exhibition.

Professors Tsunejiro Tomita of Peer's College and Eisei Maeda of the First Higher School, Tokio, gave an exhibition of jiu-jitsu, or jiu-do, as it is now termed, before Columbia University students last evening. The physical culture side was first developed and then the art as applied to self defense was demonstrated. Professor Tomita had little difficulty in flinging his Jap assistant in any manner he pleased, but it seemed that the assistant was almost a too willing subject. The holds did not seem to warrant the falls.

It was hoped by the students to see one of the university wrestlers tackle the Jap, but unfortunately no one could be found and so Keyes, one of the "gym" instructors, consented to act. He did not know the first principles of wrestling and was easily thrown; in fact, he did not put up any resistance. The opinion was that any good wrestler could have tossed the little man from Tokio about in lively style. When the Japs visited West Point Tifton had little difficulty in overcoming jiu-jitsu, and Naething, it is alleged, at the New York Athletic Club some time ago threw the Jap and sat on him.

When the Jap showed how to overcome a foe, who used a three foot sword against his weapon, which is about a foot long, the audience thought it the climax of the ridiculous. One student remarked, "Next he will show us how to catch bullets with our mouths."

The Brooklyn Daily Eagle
Wednesday March 22nd 1905

Jiu-jitsu at Columbia

Students Not Favorably Impressed With Exhibition

Professors Tsunejiro Tomita of Peer's College and Eisei Maeda of the First Higher School, Tokio, gave an exhibition of Jiu-jitsu, or Jiu-do, as it is now termed, before Columbia University students last evening. The physical culture side was first developed and then the art as applied to self-defense was demonstrated. Professor Tomita had little difficulty in flinging his Japanese assistant in any manner he pleased, but it seemed that the assistant was almost too willing a subject. The holds did not seem to warrant the falls.

It was hoped by the students that one of the university wrestlers would tackle the men, but unfortunately no one could be found and Keyes, one of the "gym" instructors consented to act. He did not know the first thing about the principles of wrestling and was easily thrown: in fact, he did not put up any good resistance. The opinion was that any good wrestler could have tossed the little man from Tokio about in a lively style. When the Japanese visited West Point Tifton had little difficulty overcoming Jiu-jitsu, and Nathan, it is alleged at the New York Athletic Club some time ago, threw the Japanese and sat on him.

When the Japanese showed how to overcome a foe who used a 3-foot sword against his weapon, which was about a foot long, the audience thought it the climax of the ridiculous. One student remarked "Next he will show us how to catch bullets with our mouths."

Chicago Tribune
Tuesday March 28th 1905

'AY,' MARCH 28, 1905.

CHARITY MEET COMES TONIGHT.

Biggest Indoor Athletic Event to Inaugurate Work of the I. A. C.

COLISEUM TO BE FILLED.

Great Crowd Will Watch Best of Amateur Athletes in Competition.

Before the initial pop of the starter's pistol is heard tonight at the Coliseum, the New Illinois Athletic club can be credited with a triumph, and it is hoped athletic success will be the medium of a big financial score for the Children's Memorial hospital.

When at 6 o'clock tonight the athletes toe the line in the preliminary heats it will mark the beginning of the biggest indoor meet in the history of athletics, and, with true Chicago modesty, it may be said the best. Weeks of well directed effort have resulted in the production of a leviathan affair to which even the imagination of a circus press agent hardly could do justice.

The New Illinois Athletic club has been able to corral a grand array of talent, and the athletic loving public is well aware of the fact. The demand for seats has been enormous, and by 8 o'clock, when the regular program will begin, there hardly will be a vacant seat left.

Interest in Shotput.

Interest will center in the meeting of Ralph Rose and W. Coe in the sixteen pound shotput, especially as the "cherry circle" representative yesterday threw the missile 51 feet 5 inches in practice. Using the same weight he used in making the world's record in the Olympian games at St. Louis, Rose several times made 50 feet, and then, going to the roof of the building, got 50 feet on his first outdoor effort. Setting himself at the second attempt, he sent the sphere 51 feet 5 inches, the best put ever recorded. Putting in such form as this has given the big Californian every confidence of his ability to beat Coe easily, as he figures Coe at his best cannot do more than 48 feet. He will use his own shot, which will be weighed and inspected, so that he will get credit for whatever performance he may accomplish. Rose, it appears, had some trouble with the Boston A. C. on account of an expense bill while there and seems anxious on this account to win from the Massachusetts man.

Work on Running Track.

Work on the building progressed all day, and many tons of black earth were spread and rolled over the bottom layer of clay. The construction of the takeoff for the pole vault has been personally superintended by Dr. Raycroft, and his suggestions have been approved by President Thompson. All contestants in this event have been asked to bring indoor spiked shoes in order to reduce the chances of accident.

Prof. T. Tomita and his assistant, E. Meada, arrived from New York last night and had some suggestions to make regarding the platform on which they will give their exhibition of jiu jitsu.

Sterling P. Wiley of the C. A. A., clerk of events, is a disciplinarian and promises that the events shall be run off on time. Contestants who are late probably will find themselves left.

The program resembles the mail order catalogue of a wholesale house, and those intending to take home more than one should bring a light porter.

Order of Events.

The preliminaries, of which there will be a large number, will be started at 6 o'clock. At 8 o'clock the regular program will begin, the field events coming in the following order: 60 yard dash, 60 yard low hurdle, 1 mile handicap, 60 yard high hurdle, two 1 mile relay races for grammar schools, 220 yard handicap, high school relay, academy relay, 880 yard run, military relay, 440 yard run, Y. M. C. A. relay, 2 mile handicap, university relay, open relay.

The field events will proceed at the same time, in this order: Tug of war, potato race, pole vault handicap, high jump, 12 pound shot, broad jump, 16 pound shot.

Chicago Tribune
Tuesday March 28th 1905

- *Biggest Indoor Athletic Event to Inaugurate work of the IAC*
- *Coliseum to be Filled*
- *Great Crowd Will Watch Best of Amateur Athletes in Competition*

Before the initial pop of the starter's pistol is heard tonight at the Coliseum, the new Illinois's Athletic Club can be credited with a triumph, and it is hoped athletic success will be the medium of a big financial score for the children's Memorial Hospital.

When at 6:00 o'clock tonight the athletes toe the line in the preliminary heats it will mark the beginning of the biggest indoor meet in the history of athletics, and, with true Chicago modesty, it may be said the best. Weeks of well-directed efforts have resulted in the production of a leviathan affair to which even the imagination of a circus press agent hardly could do justice. The new Illinois's Athletic Club has been able to corral a grand array of talent, and the athletic loving public is well aware of the fact. The demand for seats has been enormous, and by 8:00 o'clock, when the regular program begins, there will hardly be a vacant seat left.

Interest in shotput.

Interest will center in the meeting of Ralph Rose and W. Coe in the 16-pound shot put, especially as the "cherry circle" representative yesterday through the missile 51 feet 5 inches in practice. Using the same weight, he used in making the world record in The Olympian games at Saint Louis, rose several times made 50 feet, and then going to the roof of the building, got 50 feet on his first outdoor effort. Setting himself at the second attempt, he sent the sphere 51 feet 5 inches, the best putt ever recorded. Putting in such form as this has given the big Californian every confidence of his ability to beat Coe easily, as he figures Coe at his best cannot do more than 48 feet. He will use his own shot, which will be weighed and inspected, so that he will get credit for whatever performance he may accomplish. Rose, it appears, had some trouble with the

Boston A.C. on account of an expense bill while there and seems anxious on this account to win from the Massachusetts man.

Work on the Running Track

Work on the building progressed all day, and many tons of black earth were spread and rolled over the bottom layer of clay. The construction of the takeoff where the pole vault competition will be held has been personally supervised by Dr. Raycroft, and his suggestions have all been approved by President Thompson. All contestants in this event have been asked to bring indoor spiked shoes in order to reduce the chance of accident.

Professor T. Tomita and his Assistant E. Maeda arrived from New York last night and had some suggestions to make regarding the platform on which they will give their exhibition of Jiu-jitsu.

Order of events

The preliminaries, of which there will be a large number, will start at 6:00 o'clock. At 8:00 o'clock the regular program will begin, with the field events coming in the following order: 60-yard dash, 60-yard low hurdle, one mile handicap, 60-yard high hurdle, two 1-mile relay races for grammar schools, 220 yard handicap, high school relay, academy relay, 880 yard run, military relay, 440 yard run, YMCA relay, two mile handicap, university relay, open relay.

The field events will proceed at the same time, in this order: tug of war, potato race, pole vault, handicap, high jump, 12-pound shot, broad jump, 16-pound shot.

The Times Dispatch Sunday April 2nd 1905

JIU-JITSU, ART OF SELF-DEFENSE

Japanese Expert Corrects Misunderstandings and Tells What It Really Is.

SUPERIOR TO OTHER SYSTEMS

Says Result of Contest at West Point Was Much Exaggerated. The Japanese Ideal.

(Special to The Times-Dispatch.)

NEW YORK, April 1.—Those parts of modern jiu-jitsu or jiu-do, as it is now generally called in Japan, which relate especially to physical culture, were explained and practically demonstrated this week in Earl Hall, Columbia, by Prof. T. Tomita, of the Peers' College of Tokio, assisted by Prof. E. Maeda, of the first higher school, also of Tokio. In introducing the instructors, Prof. Meylan, of Columbia, said jiu-jitsu was an art of great vogue in Japan at the time of the Samurai, the noble fighters of the middle ages, but that it became practically extinct with the end of the feudal period.

It has been revived in the last fifteen years with new methods, under the name of jiu-do, and while Japan has adopted in its schools some of the American methods of physical culture, efforts are now being made in the United States to have the Japanese art adopted for physical training, as it is considered to be more advanced than fencing and boxing. The Japanese professors gave an illustration of the elementary theories of jiu-do, followed by an illustration of how to fall without injury. They also showed different falls and ways of throwing an opponent, after which Prof. Tomita gave explanatory details of the practice. Mentioning jiu-do in connection with wrestling, he said the rules are different here and in Japan, as in America a bout is over when one of the opponents touches the ground with both shoulders, while in Japan the bout is over only when one of the opponents is put out of business—that is, when placed in such a position that he has to give in because unable to move. Further demonstration was given of jiu-do as an art of self-defense, both against an armed adversary and an unarmed one.

The demonstrations were received with enthusiastic applause and it is probable one of the Japanese professors will be asked to remain permanently in New York as an instructor of jiu-do.

What Expert Says.

Mr. Yae Kichi Yabe, an authority on jiu-jitsu, as it is most widely known in this country, when interviewed in regard of jiu-jitsu and the American system of catch-as-catch-can wrestling, says.

"Jiu-jitsu is not wrestling; it is not designed for exhibitions or to amuse the public; it is a system of self-defense and of physical and moral training. There is very little similarity between jiu-jitsu and other systems of self-defense or wrestling. Jiu-jitsu aims to overcome brute strength with skill and science; it compensates for superior strength and muscular development. Its practicability as a means of self-defense has been too often demonstrated to be questioned, but as to whether a knowledge of jiu-jitsu will enable a man to defeat an American wrestler or boxer in the prize-ring may never be demonstrated, because a jiu-jitsian would not be permitted to employ any of the vital touches or arm breaking processes which enabled the ancient Samurai to defend himself unarmed against any assailant. If you place a prize-fighter in the ring and say to him you shall not deliver any knockout blows, you can only spar, and at the same time give his opponent the privilege of employing every means known to his art to defeat the prize-fighter, the result is inevitable. Of this I am certain. If any American wrestler or prize-fighter will permit himself to be locked in a room with a Japanese expert in jiu-jitsu and each employ their own methods, the Japanese will carry out the inert form of his opponent on his shoulders in ten minutes.

"There have recently been many contests between self-termed Japanese experts and American athletes, and in many cases the latter are claiming the victory, but I have yet to learn of any real expert in the art who has met defeat at the hands of an American wrestler. The result of the contest at West Point between Mr. Tomita and three of West Point's best all-round athletes has been greatly exaggerated by the American press. The apparent defeat of Mr. Tomita was not a defeat from the jiu-jitsian's view-point. He went to West Point to give exhibitions in jiu-jitsu, not to challenge their best men to a contest of strength and skill. His assistant, a Japanese, sustained a slight injury, which made it necessary for Mr. Tomita to call for volunteers; three able fellows responded. The first one, in his eagerness to overcome the Japanese by sheer brute force, received a sprained ankle; the second one fared but little better; the third one, "Bull" Tipton, the famous West Point quarterback (an all-round athlete who weighs two hundred pounds, and is trained to the minute), rushed the one-hundred and five-pound Japanese to the mat, and the spectators and public press applauded. As a matter of fact Mr. Tomita, who is past forty years of age, and weighs just one hundred and five pounds, attempted to enforce a submission by falling to the floor and carrying the body of his opponent over his head and shoulders. In this he was unsuccessful, but is it to be wondered at? Where will you find a man of one hundred and five pounds' weight, who by employing a knowledge of any science of self-defense, can defeat an opponent of twice his weight and strength without injuring or disabling him? Had Mr. Tomita permitted himself to employ a vital touch the result would have been different, but to do this in a friendly contest would bring disfavor and dishonor on his head.

The Japanese Ideal.

"The American public have not forgotten that Mr. Higashi, the jiu-jitsu expert who weighs one hundred and thirty pounds, put out three of the best men in the New York police department in less than fifteen minutes, and yet, because some self-styled experts have accepted challenges from American wrestlers to a public contest and have been defeated, there are those who believe that jiu-jitsu is not superior to the American system of wrestling; others are dangerous for a public contest between an acknowledged jiu-jitsu expert and an American wrestler as if the jiu-jitsians were a class of men who could be reduced to the rank or vocation of prize-fighting, for public entertainment or pecuniary gain. Such an idea would never be tolerated by a jiu-jitsian who has the high sense of honor and true moral discipline of his forefathers. To the Japanese, jiu-jitsu is associated with the loftiest sentiment, for it is the instrument which trains both mind and body and fits the young generation to bear the responsibilities of manhood. No Japanese is worthy of the name of a jiu-jitsian who uses the art for any other purpose than enforcing justice or defending his honor and person."

- **Jiu-jitsu Art of Self Defense**
- **Japanese Expert Corrects Misunderstandings and Tells What it Really Is**
- **Superior to Other Systems**
- **Says Result of Contest at West Point was Much Exaggerated.**
- **The Japanese ideal.**

Those parts of modern Jiu-jitsu or Judo as it is now generally called in Japan which relate especially to physical culture, were explained and practically demonstrated this week in Earl Hall, Columbia, by Professor T. Tomita of the Peers College of Tokyo. He is assisted by Professor E. Maeda of the First Higher School also of Tokyo. In introducing the instructors, Professor Meylan, of Colombia, said Jiu-jitsu was an art in great vogue in Japan at the time of the Samurai, the noble fighters of the Middle Ages, but that it became practically extinct with the end of the feudal period.

It has been revived in the last 50 years with new methods under the name of Judo, and while Japan has adopted it in its schools, some of the American methods of physical culture [are also being adopted.] Efforts are now being made in the United States to have the Japanese art adopted for physical training, as it is considered more advanced than fencing and boxing.

The Japanese professors gave an illustration of the elementary theories of Judo, followed by an illustration of how to fall without injury. They also showed different falls and ways of throwing an opponent, after which Professor Tomita gave explanatory details of the practice. Mentioning judo in connection with wrestling, he said "The rules are different here and in Japan. In America, a match is over when one of the opponents touches the ground with both shoulders, while in Japan the bout is over only when one of the opponents is put out of business=that is, when placed in such a position that he has to give in because unable to move."

A further demonstration was given of Judo as an art of self-defense, both against an armed adversary and an unarmed one.

The demonstrations were received with enthusiastic applause, and it is probable one of the Japanese professors will be asked to remain permanently in New York as an instructor of Judo.

What experts say

Mr. Yae Kichi Yabe, an authority on Jiu-jitsu, as it is most widely known in this country, when interviewed in regard of Jiu-jitsu and the American system of catch-as-catch-can wrestling, says,

"Jiu-jitsu is not wrestling it is not designed for exhibitions or to amuse the public. It is a system of self-defense and a physical and moral training period there is very little similarity between Jiu-jitsu and other systems of self-defense or wrestling. Jiu-jitsu aims to overcome brute strength with skill and science: it compensates for superior strength and muscular development. Its practicability as a means of self-defense has been too-often demonstrated to be questioned. But as to whether a knowledge of Jiu-jitsu will enable a Japanese man to defeat an American wrestler or boxer in the prize ring may never be demonstrated, because a Jiu-jitsian would not be permitted to employ any of the vital touches or arm breaking processes which enabled the ancient Samurai to defend himself unarmed against any assailant."

"If you place a prize fighter in the ring and say to him *you shall not deliver any knockout blows, you can only spar*, and, at the same time give his opponent the privilege of employing every means known to his art to defeat the prize fighter, the result is inevitable. Of this I am certain, if any American wrestler or prize fighter will permit himself to be locked in a room with a Japanese expert in Jiu-jitsu and each employ their own methods, the Japanese will carry out the inert form of his opponents on his shoulder in 10 minutes."

"There have recently been many contests, between self-termed Japanese experts and American athletes, and in many cases the latter are claiming victory, but I have yet to learn of any *real* expert in the art who has met defeat at the hands of an American wrestler. The result of the contest at West Point between Mr. Tomita and three of West point's best all-round athletes has been greatly exaggerated by the American press. The apparent defeat of Mr. Tomita was not a defeat from the Jiu-jisian's view-point. He went to West Point to give exhibitions and Jiu-jitsu, not to challenge their best men in contest of strength and skill. His assistant, a Japanese, sustained a slight injury which made it necessary for Mr. Tomita to call for volunteers: three able fellows responded. The first one, in his eagerness to overcome the Japanese by sheer brute force, received a sprained ankle. The second one fared but little better. The third one, "Bull" Tipton (Arthur Charles "Bull" Tipton 1882~1942,) the famous West Point quarterback an all-round athlete who weighs two hundred pounds and is trained to the minute, rushed the 105-pound Japanese to the mat, and the spectators and public press applauded."

"As a matter of fact, Mr. Tomita, who is past 40 years of age and weighs just 105 pounds, attempted to enforce a submission by falling to the floor and carrying the body of his opponent over his head and shoulders. In this he was unsuccessful, but is it to be wondered at? Where will you find a man of 105 pounds weights, who by employing a knowledge of any science that or self-defense, can defeat an opponent of twice his weight and strength without injuring or disabling him? Had Mr. Tomita permitted himself to employ a vital touch the result would have been different, but to do this in a friendly contest would bring disfavor and dishonor on his head."

The Japanese ideal

"The American public have not forgotten that Mr. Higashi, the Jiu-jitsu expert who weighs 130 pounds, put out three of the best men in New York Police department in less than 15 minutes, and yet, because some self-styled experts have accepted challenges from American wrestlers to a public contest and have been defeated, there are those that believe that Jiu-jitsu is not superior to the American system of wrestling cold and others are clamoring for a public contest between and acknowledged Jiu-jitsu experts and an American wrestler as if the Jiu-jitsians were a class of men who could be reduced to the rank or vocation of prize fighting for public entertainment or pecuniary gain."

"Such an idea would never be tolerated by a Jiu-jitsian who has the high sense of honor and true moral discipline of his forefather's period to the Japanese, Jiu-jitsu is associated with the loftiest sentiment, for it is the instrument which trains both mind and body and fits the young generation to bear the responsibility of manhood. No Japanese is worthy of the name of a Jiu-jitsian who uses the art for any other purpose than enforcing justice or defending his honor and person."

The Topeka Daily Herald
Monday April 3rd 1905

IT BEATS JIU-JITSU

New Form of Wrestling which is Warranted Not to Injure.

New York, April 3.—Two little nut-brown men from the land of the Mikado threw each other around Columbia university's gymnasium last night before a crowd of students. The little men demonstrate that "jiu-do" is an improvement upon jiu-jitsu.

The two wrestlers, whose muscles seemed to be abruptly absent when they weren't in motion, were Prof. T. Tomita, of the Peers' college, of Tokio, and Prof. E. Naeda, of the First Higher school, of Tokio. Dr. Takanine made as adequate explanatory remarks as he could while the demonstration was going on. The Japs worked with such rapidity that none could tell exactly how the tricks were done. Mr. Tomita yanked Mr. Naeda toward him and then, scornful like, threw him away, Mr. Naeda bringing up against the wall.

Then Mr. Naeda came back for more, and playfully jerked Mr. Tomita's arm almost out of its socket. In the middle of the strenuous seance, while Mr. Tomita was kiting through the air, a rugged student was lured into the battlefield and induced to wrestle. In three minutes he was presented with three falls, and tottered from the scene of action.

The idea of jiu-do is to give and take falls without injury. The little nut-brown men fell in a heap, like a ball, and rolled over and over. Their heads never touched the ground. Their bodies never met while in combat. Only the arms and hands, maeuvered dexterously, were called into play.

HOLD-UP FRUSTRATED

Lynzville, Wis., April 3.—John Watson, driver of a stage, today frustrated a hold-up by driving away from two masked men. Their bullets broke the glass in the coach. No one was injured. William Hoard, a lumber dealer of Eastman, had $40,000 in his pockets.

The Topeka Daily Herald
Monday April 3rd 1905

It beats Jiu-jitsu
New form of wrestling which is warranted not to injure

Two little nut-brown men from the island of the Mikado threw each other around Columbia University's gymnasium last night before a crowd of students. The little men demonstrated that Jiu-do is an improvement upon Jiu-jitsu.

The two wrestlers, whose muscles seem to be abruptly absent when they weren't in motion, were Professor Tomita, of the Peer's college, of Tokio, and Professor E. Maeda of the First Higher School, of Tokio. Doctor Takanine made as adequate explanatory remarks as he could while the demonstration was going on. The Japanese worked with such rapidity that none could tell exactly how the tricks were done. Mr. Tomita yanked Mr. Maeda toward him and then, scornful like, threw him away, Mr. Maeda banging up against the wall.

Then Mr. Maeda came back for more, and playfully jerked Mr. Tomita's arm almost out of its socket. In the middle of the strenuous seance, while Mr. Tomita was kiting through the air, a rugged student was lured into the battlefield and induced to wrestle. In three minutes, he was presented with three falls, and tottered from the scene of action.

The idea of Jiu-do is to give and take falls without injury. The little nut-brown men fell over in a heap like a ball, and rolled over and over. Their heads never touched the ground. Their bodies never met while in combat. Only the arms and hands, maneuvered dexterously, were called into play.

Hold up frustrated.

John Watson, driver of a stage, today frustrated a holdup by driving away from two masked men. Their bullets broke the glass of the coach. No one was injured. William Hoard, a lumber dealer of Eastman, had $40,000 in his pocket.

Gazette News : Tuesday April 5th 1905

FRISBEE-ONO CONTEST

All Arrangements Made for the Wrestling Match in Asheville on Thursday.

The wrestling match between Tom Frisbee of Madison county, and Professor A. Ono of Japan, at the Auditorium next Friday evening, August 4, is now an assured fact after several days of negotiations. Money---cold cash---to assure the match was placed in the hands of J. E. Rankin, cashier of the Battery Park bank this morning and all conferences are at an end. Mr. Rankin has $400. Professor Ono deposited $100 as a forfeit, payable to Sheriff Reed, Ben Barnes and D. G. Noland, under whose management the bout will be pulled off, if he fails to appear in the ring on the night of August 4 while the managers have deposited $300 with Mr. Rankin to secure Professor Ono. Mr. Frisbee has given his check for $100 to the managers as a forfeit for failure to appear in the ring, and the managers have given Mr. Frisbee a $300 guarantee for the fulfilment of their contract.

With the exception of a few minor changes insisted on by Professor Ono, the bout will be pulled off under the rules and regulations agreed upon Sunday between the two men. Mr. Carrier, who was selected by Professor Ono as his referee and Mr. Roberts, selected by Mr. Frisbee, will not referee the contest but instead a professional referee will be secured from one of the large cities to come here and be at the ring side in an official capacity. The wrestle will be best two out of three and interest in the approaching contest is manifest on all sides. It is probable that a special train will be operated from Marshall on August 4 to accommodate the large number of Madson county men who will be on hand to witness the bout.—Gazette-News.

Gazette News
Tuesday April 5th 1905

FRISBEE-ONO CONTEST
All arrangements made for the wrestling match in Asheville on Thursday.

The wrestling match between Tom Frisbee of Madison County and Professor A. Ono of Japan at the auditorium next Friday evening August 4th is now an assured fact after several days of negotiations. Money, cold cash, to assure the match was placed in the hands of J.E. Rankin, cashier of the Battery Park bank this morning and all conferences are at an end. Mr. Rankin has $400. Professor Ono offered $300 as a forfeit payable to sheriff Reed. Ber Barnes and D.G. Noland, under whose management the bout will be pulled off., will be paid that money if he fails to appear in the ring on the night of August 4th. While the managers have deposited $300 with Mr. Rankin to secure Professor Ono, Mr. Frisbee has given his check for $100 to the managers as a forfeit for failure to appear in the ring, and the managers have given Mr. Frisbee a $300 guarantee for the fulfilment of their contract.

With the exception of a few minor changes insisted on by Professor Ono, the bout will be pulled off under the rules and regulations agreed upon Sunday between the two men. Mr. Carrier, who was selected by Professor Ono as his referee and Mr. Roberts, selected by Mr. Frisbee, will not referee the contest but instead a professional referee will be secured from one of the large cities to come here and be at the ringside in an official capacity.

The wrestle will be best two out of three and interest in the approaching contest is manifest on all sides. It is probable that a special train will be operated from Marshall on August 4th to accommodate the large number of Madison County men who will be on hand to witness the belt.

Buffalo Evening News Monday, April 10, 1905

THE GENTLE ART OF JIU-DO

Resembles Jiu-Jitsu, But Is Not Intended as a Means of Self Defense.

EXHIBITED AT COLUMBIA UNIVERSITY

Marvelous Control of Muscles Displayed—Art of Failing Properly Illustrated.

A new thing in the line of Japanese athletics and physical culture was shown last week at Columbia. Prof. T. Tomita of the Peers' College, Tokio, demonstrated the gentle art of "jiu-do," which is declared to resemble jiu-jitsu only as a sort of grandson. Jiu-do is a physical culture thing, and, primarily, has little to do with self-defence, which is the sole object of the jiu-jitsu. The demonstration of the new art was made before a large crowd of instructors and students in the gymnasium. Prof. Tomita introduced the science as one having authority. He learned it from the originator, who developed the thing only about 35 years ago, reports the New York Sun.

Prof. Tomita and his assistant, Prof. E. Maeda, both of whom are finely built little men, came out on the floor dressed in complete habiliments of white silk. Their shoes were perhaps the most peculiar things they wore. These were made of very soft leather, and had a separate part for the great toe. They buttoned up the back, rather curiously. The trousers they wore were only to the knee, and were gathered like bloomers. The blouses had wide lapels, which were used later in some of the tricks to get a hold.

Wonderful Wrestling Trick.

Prof. Bashford Dean, who has been in Japan, told the audience something about the art of jiu-do, and then the Japanese entered to illustrate. The first part of the programme consisted in showing some of the exercise to obtain control of the muscles, which is one of the chief things. Some wonderful things in the line of muscle-moving were done. Then followed a little exposition of some of the things in which the art is allied to jiu-jitsu. Several grips and holds were worked through slowly to give the persons present an idea of how the things were done. Then Prof. Tomita worked them through with lightning speed on his unfortunate assistant, who came up smiling and polite but purple of visage after each trick. A number of the wrestling tricks were tried on Mr. Keith, one of the Columbia gymnasium instructors, who was almost choked to the suffocating point by one of them.

An Amusing Feature.

"The art of falling properly," was then taken up in its turn. The professor showed how falling should be done so as not to hurt one's self. He ran about 10 yards, suffered his attendant to trip him, and then fell wrongly, just to show what a nerve-jarring and bone-racking thing it is to fall improperly. Then he tried it all over again and fell properly. This feature of the programme was a decided novelty, and was much appreciated by the onlookers. So pleased was the professor at his success that he fell all sorts of ways, backward and forward, invariably landing in some way so as to ease the shock and save his bones.

The programme was brought to a close with an exhibition of mediaeval jiu-jitsu, which was intended for the protection of an unarmed man against an armed antagonist. Prof. Maeda armed himself with a sword, while Prof. Tomita contented himself with carrying a fan, folded tightly. The two strolled on to the mat from opposite directions and began a lively pantomime of quarreling. Then followed queer Japanese disputations, not unlike the tearing of Irish linen in sound. This ended suddenly, when Prof. Maeda made a savage swipe at his antagonist with the hooked sword. Tomita was right there, however, and dodged under the arc of the swinging blade. In something less than it takes to tell he had swung his fan so sharply on Maeda's hand that the latter dropped his sword. Then Tomita got a jiu-do grip on his rival and had him hors du combat in a jiffy.

A Misunderstanding.

Prof. Tomita said that there had been considerable misunderstanding as to the exact nature of jiu-jitsu and jiu-do. The recent events at West Point, in which Higashi was thrown around easily by several of the cadets, were taken to mean that the Japanese style of wrestling was worthless. Tomita said that Higashi did not understand that it meant anything to be thrown on one's back. According to the Japanese style, only when a man is pinioned in any way so that he cannot move is he beaten. The misunderstanding as to this made it easy for the West Pointers to down Higashi, according to the American system. He did not try to avoid it, and was perplexed to know what they were trying it for. Tomita was sure things would have been different had Higashi known that he should try to avoid being thrown on his back.

The Jury Dodger.

A juror came before a Supreme Court judge in Brooklyn with a certificate that he was incapacitated for jury duty by deafness. The certificate was vouched in the most technical of medical phraseology, and the judge gravely read it through while the afflicted juror stood by, his hand behind his ear, in an attitude of pained attention. Finally the judge looked up and said softly: "I'm sorry for you, sir, you can go—"

"Thank you," said the delighted juror, starting to leave the platform.

"—back and sit down!" roared His Honor, "where you will be in readiness to act as a trial juror in this court. This certificate is a lie."—Leslie's Magazine.

Buffalo Evening News
Monday, April 10, 1905

Resembles Jiu-jitsu, But Is Not Intended as a Means of Self Defense
Exhibited at Columbia University
Marvelous Control of Muscles Displayed – Art of Falling Properly Illustrated

A new thing in Japanese athletics and physical culture was shown last week at Columbia. Professor T. Tomita of the Peers college Tokio demonstrated the gentle art of "jiu-do" which is declared to resemble Jiu-jitsu only as a sort of grandson. Jiu-do is primarily a physical culture thing and primarily has little to do with self-defense, which is the soul object of the Jiu-jitsu. The demonstration of the new art was made before a large crowd of instructors and students in the gymnasium. Professor Tomita introduced the science as one having authority. He learned it from the originator who developed the thing only about 35 years ago, reports the New York Sun.

Prof. Tomita and his assistant, Prof. E. Maeda, both of whom are finely built little men, came out on the floor dressed in complete habiliments of white silk. Their shoes were perhaps the most peculiar things they wore. These were made of very soft leather, and they had a separate part for the great toe. They buttoned up the back, rather curiously. The trousers they wore were only to the knee, and were gathered like bloomers. The blouses had wide lapels, which were used later in some of the tricks to get a hold.

Wonderful Wrestling Trick

Professor Bashford Dean, who has been in Japan, told the audience something about the art of judo, and then the Japanese entered to illustrate. The first part of the program consisted in showing some of the exercises to obtain control of the muscles, which is one of the chief things. Some wonderful things in the line of muscle moving were done. Then followed a little exposition of some of the things in which the art is allied to Jiu-jitsu. Several grips and holds were worked through slowly to give the person present an idea of how the things were done. Then Prof. Tomita worked them through with lightning speed on his unfortunate assistant, who came up smiling and polite, but purple of visage after each trick. A number of the wrestling tricks were tried on Mr. Keith, one of the Columbia gymnasium instructors, who was almost choked to the suffocating point by one of them.

An Amusing Feature

"The art of falling properly" was then taken up in its turn. The professor showed how falling should be done so as not to hurt oneself. He ran about 10 yards, suffered his attendant to trip him, and then fell wrongly just to show what a nerve jarring and bone wracking thing it is to fall improperly. Then he tried it all over again and fell properly. This feature of the program was a decided novelty and was much appreciated by the onlookers. So pleased was the professor at his success that he fell all sorts of ways, backward and forward, invariably landing in some way so as to ease the shock and save his bones."

"The program was brought to a close with an exhibition of medieval Jiu-jitsu, which was intended for the protection of an unarmed man against an armed antagonist. Professor Maeda armed himself with a sword, while Professor Tomita contented himself with carrying a fan, folded tightly."

"The two strolled on to the mat from opposite directions and began a lively pantomime of quarreling. Then followed queer Japanese disputations, not unlike the tearing of Irish linen in sound. This ended suddenly, when Professor Maeda made a savage swipe at his antagonist with the hooked sword."

"Professor Tomita was right there, however, and dodged under the arc of the swinging blade in something less than it takes to tell, and he had swung his fan so sharply on Maeda's sword hand that the latter dropped his sword. Then Tomita got a Judo grip on his rival had him hors de combat in a jiffy."

A Misunderstanding

Professor Tomita said that there had been a considerable misunderstanding as to the exact nature of Jiu-jitsu and judo. The recent events at West Point, in which Higashi was thrown around easily by several of the cadets, were taken to mean that Japanese style wrestling was worthless. Professor Tomita said that Higashi did not understand that it meant anything to be thrown on one's back. According to the Japanese style only when a man is pinioned in anyway so that he cannot move is he beaten. The misunderstanding as to this made it easy for the West Pointers to down Higashi, according to the American system. He did not try to avoid it, and was perplexed to know what they were trying it for. Tomita was sure things would have been different had he actually known he should try to avoid being thrown on his back.

The Jury Dodger

A juror came before a Supreme Court judge in Brooklyn with a certificate that he was incapacitated for jury duty by deafness. The certificate was vouched in the most technical of medical phraseology, and the judge gravely read it through while the afflicted juror stood by, his hand behind his ear in an attitude of pained attention. Finally, the judge looked up and said softly: "I'm sorry for you, Sir, you can go-"

"Thank you," said the delighted juror starting to leave the platform.

"-back and sit down!" Roared His Honor. "Where you will be in readiness to act as a trial juror in this court. This certificate is a lie."
-Leslie's Magazine

The Pittsburgh Press
Wednesday May 17th 1905

JIU JITSU EXPERT TO INSTRUCT U. S. CADETS

Prof. Ono, Japan's Greatest Exponent of the Art Is Going to West Point to Become an Instructor at the Military Academy

San Francisco, May 17. — Prof. Ono, Japan's greatest exponent of the art of jiu jitsu, who arrived here recently en route to West Point, where he will teach the young idea at the military academy how to twist an adversary into a state of insensibility, is a man of tremendous strength and remarkable quickness. It is said of him that he can break a man's neck with a slight push with the open hand and the dislocating of an arm or a leg by a gentle twist negotiated with two fingers is mere child's play. Ono waded through all of the strong men of Hawaii on his way over, disposing of six men in as many minutes.

Akitaro Ono and Masoaki Tauimoto in their Jiu-Jitsu Act

The Pittsburgh Press
Wednesday May 17th 1905

Jiu Jitsu Expert to Instruct U.S. Cadets

Professor Ono, Japan's greatest exponent of the art is going to West Point to become an instructor at the Military Academy

Professor Ono, Japan's greatest exponent of the art of Jiu-jitsu who arrived here recently en-route to West Point, where he will teach the sound idea at the Military Academy of how to twist and adversary into a state of insensibility. He's a man of tremendous strength and remarkable quickness. It is said of him that he can break a man's neck with a slight push with the open hand and that the dislocating of an arm or leg by a gentle twist negotiated with two fingers is mere child's play. Ono waded through all of the strong men of Hawaii on his way over, disposing of six men in as many minutes.

Ashville Citizen Times
Sunday June 30, 1905

Ashville Citizen Times
Sunday June 30, 1905

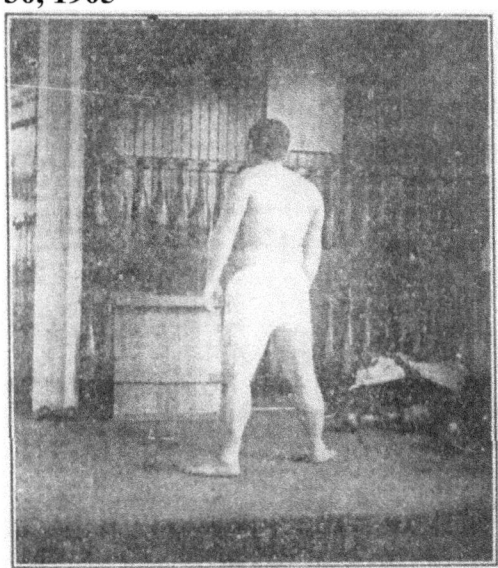

Championship wrestling belt auditorium, Friday evening, August 4th

Between big Tom Frisbee, world champion and professor A. Ono, Jiu-jitsu expert from Japan.

Professor Ono, a Japanese expert Jiu-jitsu wrestler and a member of a royal family, will meet big Tom Frisbee of Madison County North Carolina and wrestle for the championship two best out of three belts.

Big Tom is one of Professor Muldoon's experts and was trained in New York and has never been defeated in a wrestling match, and says that he feels sure that he can demonstrate to the people that the art of Jiu-jitsu is not superior to that of ours. He weighs 304 pounds he's six feet five and a half inches high and is well proportioned in every respect and will be hard to handle with the art of Jiu-jitsu or otherwise.

Prices $0.75 to $2   Apply to DG Newland for boxes
Tickets on sale Monday at Plaffin's
A preliminary belt will be given by two of Professor Ono's trainers

The Omaha Daily News
Saturday August 5th 1905

Jap Throws Carolina Giant

Jiu-jitsu expert defeats Ashville man at wrestling

    Professor Ono, Japanese instructor of Jiu-jitsu at Annapolis, and "Big Tom" Frisbee indulged in a wrestling match at this city last night.
The Jap was the victor. Frisbee weighs 305 pounds, and is 6 feet and 5 1/2 inches. Ono weighs 207 pounds and stands 5 feet 6 1/2 inches Two thousand people were present to see the match.

The Brooklyn Daily Eagle
Friday August 18th 1905

JAP PRESS AGENT GETS BUSY.

Says Young Piening "Bited His Lips" and Challenged Maeda—Match To-morrow Night.

A wrestling bout between "Young" Piening and Professor Maeda, the jiu-jitsu expert, will be decided at Manhattan Beach to-morrow and the Japanese press agent has been busy. Here is his advance notice of the match:

"A POPULAR AMERICAN CHAMPION-WRESTLER WILL MEET WITH A NOTED JAPANESE JU-JITSU EXPERT AT 'PARADISE OF JAPAN,' MANHATTAN BEACH, ON NEXT SATURDAY EVENING, $3,000 BET.

"The question to ascertain true quality of deadly tricks of Ju-Jitsu, a wonderful Japanese art of both self-defence and offensive movement, which has already been interested the people's discussion; will no longer remain a mystery, when a formidable American champion wrestler, Oscar Dresoderi, or Young Piening or more widely known as the Brooklyn Butcher Boy, has met with a celebrated Jap Ju-Jitsu expert, Pro. E. Maeda, a national champion of Japan, and the instructor of Ju-Jitsu to Princeton University, on the ring, and challenge the contest, at 'Paradise of Japan,' Manhattan Beach, on Saturday evening, August 19th.

"The challenge has initially been made by Young Piening to race his strength with Prof. Maeda, several days ago; and it has come to a good mutual understanding after the careful but gallant negotiation. Prof. Maeda has declared to the public to have a fight with any American challenger a long time ago, but in the meantime almost no one else has ever come out as a candidate of the contest, therefore, Young Piening as gallant and dauntless as he is to be, bited his lips, and made himself to Paradise of Japan and demanded for a challenge, and emphatically declared to the mass of gaping Japs, that he is sure to overcome this Jap Ju-Jitsuist within fifteen minutes, and throw him high into the air and whirl his rice-cake body like a ball, with the mixed styles, or he will agree to forfeit three thousand dollars, lost he was defeated by that Yellow Bull-dog.

"The contest will be taken place under the special auspices of Captain Walter T. Asamy, a well-known authority on Ju-Jitsu of Japan, and the general manager to Paradise of Japan, whose capacity as a ring leader has been proved by a distinguished offering of the honorably title of vice-President to the National Athletic Association of Japan.

"Young Piening when interviewed by the reporter assured himself, in a hot high air, 'May be Jap'll be stronger than that stupid Russian, but, look here. I'm an'merican and no Jap would stand with us,' and tuned a soft, melodious whistle into the sky, if as he are sure of to be a winner.

"Prof. E. Maede, a celebrated Ju-Jitsu master in Japan, also he was an instructor to the Kodo-Kwan Ju-do School of Tokio, a famous institution for Ju-do, or art of Ju-Jitsu, whose cute stature is considerably smaller than even an average Jap in the town, and he looks no fighter at all; But when any one sees his wonderful muscle development and his steel-built frame, would doubtlessly believe of his capacity as a professional fighter. This little admirable Oriental fighter has expressed his own opinion rather sircustically. When the reporter interrogated him, he said, 'I don't know whether I win or not, as I always believe, the result of contest evidently depend upon the chance, but you can imagine the effect of the contemplated fighting between Mr. Oscar Dresoderf and me on comin' Saturday evening, when if you just remind how our great Admiral Togo has won of his tremendous naval battle without boasting himself, even a bit. Excuse me, I'm no boaster nor bluffer,' and revealed a good, innocent Peek-a-boo smile which gave a characteristic ancient impression of the chivalrous Samurai."

The Brooklyn Daily Eagle
Friday August 18th 1905
Japanese press agent gets busy

Says young Piening "bited his lips" and challenged Maeda- Match to-morrow night

A wrestling belt between "Young" Piening and Professor Maeda, the Jiu-jitsu expert, will be decided at Manhattan Beach tomorrow and the Japanese press agent has been busy. Here is his advance notice of the match:

"A popular American champion wrestler will meet with a noted Japanese Jiu-jitsu expert at 'Paradise of Japan' Manhattan Beach on next Saturday evening, $3000 bet."

"The question to ascertain true quality of deadly tricks of Jiu-jitsu, a wonderful Japanese art of both self-defense and offensive movement, which has already been interested the people's discussion; will no longer remain a mystery, when a formidable American champion wrestler, Oscar , or "Young Piening", or more widely known as the "Brooklyn Butcher Boy", will meet a celebrated Japanese Jiu-jitsu expert, Prof. E. Maeda, a national champion of Japan, and the instructor of Jiu-jitsu to Princeton University, on the ring, and challenge the contest, at Paradise of Japan, Manhattan Beach, on Saturday evening, August 19th.

"The challenge has initially been made by Young Piening to race his strength with Professor Maeda, several days ago; and it has come to a good mutual understanding after the careful but gallant negotiation. Professor Maeda has declared to the public to have a fight with any American challenger a long time ago, but in the meantime almost no one else has ever come out as a candidate of the contest, therefore, Young Piening as gallant and dauntless as he is to be, bited his lips, and made himself to Paradise of Japan and demanded for a challenge, and emphatically declared to the mass of gaping Japanese, that he is sure to overcome this Japanese Ju-jitsuist within 15 minutes, and throw him high into the air and whirl his rice-cake body like a ball, with the mixed styles, or he will agree to forfeit $3000, lest he was defeated by that yellow bulldog.

The contest will take place under the special auspices of Captain Walter T. Asamy, a well-known authority on Jiu-jitsu of Japan, and the general manager to Paradise of Japan, whose capacity as a ringleader has been proved by a distinguished offering of the honorary title of vice president of the national Athletic Association of Japan.

Young Piening when interviewed by the reporter assured himself, in a hot high air, 'May be Jap'll be stronger than that stupid Russian, but, look here. I'm an'merican and no Jap would stand with us,' and tuned a soft, melodious whistle into the sky, if as he is sure of to be a winner.

Prof. E Maeda, a celebrated Jiu-jitsu master in Japan, also he was an instructor to the Kodo-Kwan Ju-do School of Tokio, a famous institute for Jiu-do, or the art of Jiu-jitsu, who's cute stature is considerably smaller than even the average Japanese in the town, and he looks no fighter at all: But when anyone sees his wonderful muscle development and his steel built frame, would doubtlessly believe of his capacity as a professional fighter.

This little admirable oriental fighter has expressed his own opinion rather circuitously. When the reporter interrogated him, he said,

"I don't know whether I win or not, as I always believe, the result of contest event evidently depends upon the chance, but you can imagine the effect of the contemplated fighting between Mr. Oscar Dresendorf and me on comin' Saturday evening, when if you just remind how our great Admiral Togo has won his tremendous naval battle without boasting himself, even a bit. Excuse me, I'm no boaster or bluffer," and revealed a good, innocent Peek-a-boo smile which gave a characteristic ancient impression of the chivalrous Samurai.

Ashville Citizen Times
Tuesday November 7, 1905

Prof. Maeda Explains Some Features of the Art of Judo

Prof. Higeo Maeda of Japan, a graduate of the Judo Physical Culture School of Japan, is in the city, visiting Prof. Tone in his class. To a representative of The Citizen, Prof. Maeda explained several matters in connection with jiu jitsu and judo that are not well understood in this country and in the English language. Some light on the class of people engaged in teaching the art in this country. He quoted from an article by a Japanese admirer of the judo art and said:

"All Japanese are not necessarily jiu jitsu experts, just as all Americans are not necessarily wrestlers or prize fighters, or else gentlemen even. These Japanese who profess jiu jitsu in this country are not necessarily skilled to teach it, or even to say that they know much about it; just as thirty or forty years ago, when Japan was eager to secure the services of any English-speaking person to teach the language, some common soldier or even tramps from England or America were teaching English in Japan as schools. Since some foreign newspaper correspondents in Japan began to report wonderful things of the art of self-defense commonly so called outside our own country, saying that in Japan there was no man who did not study it, from the emperor down to the poorest laborer, that this universal practice of jiu jitsu was the greatest cause of Japan's victory over Russia as well as of her soldiers' health and sturdiness, and so on ad infinitum, you Americans have aroused a great deal of curiosity to see the actual thing done before your eyes, hence the result that some young Japanese, who were house work boys or school boys until the previous day, whose name even were not known among their countrymen, much less as jiu jitsu men, appear on the stage one lucky morning as great masters of the art of jitsuryu.

"Jiu jitsu was a genuine product of feudalism in Japan, and with the feudalism it practically died thirty-eight years ago when our great revolution took place. Some fifteen years later it revived under the new name of judo, after careful investigation and comparison of all the old forms or schools of jiu jitsu on the part of Prof. Kano, who has completely remodeled and enlarged the teaching on the physiological and educational basis and through whose zeal and influence this judo is now introduced into nearly all government schools over and above the accidental systems of physical training. The old jiu jitsu aimed at either killing or otherwise controlling one's foe by a mere throw without using any weapon, or preventing a criminal without inflicting wound upon him, or else keeping one's antagonist in such a position as rendered resistance impossible. As such a mode of fighting or of self-defense without weapons, it had to resort to the choking of the throat, the twisting of the joints, the kicking or hitting of the vital parts, as well as to mere forcible throws down on the ground. But the new school of judo is no longer an art of fighting or of self-defense, but a system of moral culture combined with a special form of physical training, and as our fathers sought, judo teaching differs in its aim as well as in practice from that in its old form. In the older days our practice was strongly discouraged though we tried hard to escape from these modes of attack. In this glorious country of modern machinery, we are a monopoly and some form may not be to teach jiu jitsu as an art of warfare is of course dear. Matches of jiu jitsu men versus wrestlers are no less absurd. Jiu jitsu and judo both aim at controlling the antagonist with the least expenditure possible of mere brute strength, while in wrestling, either of America or Japan, the main feature is strength more than skill or agility. Because wrestling uses much physical force, wrestlers cannot continue a match very long before they get exhausted, consequently they have to decide the case with a momentary touch of both shoulders to the floor. But in Japanese wrestling a ring of about 15 feet in diameter is used and to be pushed out of the circle even by one-half of a foot means defeat, as well as a mere touch on the ground of one finger or elbow or knee. On the contrary, in jiu jitsu matches we have to keep the opponent on the mat for a minutes or two in an invariable condition, or else we throw our antagonist for hit on the ground, and to do that that we may first tie down as a means to the end. Then, again in an accomplishment for samurai or noble-gentlemen of the feudal times, jiu jitsu presupposes that both parties are properly dressed as respectful people should be, whereas wrestling of America and also of Japan is done in a condition of nudity. From the very nature of the two things, jiu jitsu men and wrestlers cannot try their skill or strength on a footing of equality. It is something like comparing skill in running and riding.

"If, however, both parties can agree upon some fair terms by mutual compromise, matches between these two different things may not be altogether uninteresting. But you must expect the result always will be that wrestlers may beat jiu jitsu men in wrestling ways, but not in jiu jitsu ways, where, as the latter may succeed in controlling or resisting wrestlers, according to their own standard, and which wrestlers themselves may not recognize as their defeat from their own standpoint. Such being the case, Americans will not see much truth of their art, even if they beat a jiu jitsu man, for them to try a match with a noted wrestler in jiu jitsu is no more nor less than the head of it. If one must be seen such a performance to satisfy your curiosity, it may not be a bad idea for you to have a preliminary contest between old style jiu jitsu men and scientific judoists, to see whether such a man as Higashi or Yabe is really entitled or not to call themselves champions and exponents of this unique sort of gentlemanly sport of Japan. You must remember that there are at least half a dozen of true judoists on the Atlantic side of this continent, who have received certificates for their attainments direct from Prof. Kano, founder of the modern improved school of judo, by studying for years in his great gymnasium in Tokio known as the Kodaokwan, which is visited by foreign tourists as one of the rare institutions of our country."

Prof. Maeda himself was a student under Prof. Kano and believes that as a mode of physical training judo is superior to American methods of physical culture. Asked what he thought of the American style of wrestling, Prof. Maeda said he thought highly of it and admired the skill shown by American wrestlers in matches. He has himself taken part in several exhibitions in American style, but said he did not intend to engage in a match in this city.

Prof. Maeda leaves in a few days for New York, where he will take part in an exhibition the latter part of November. He will return here in December and may remain for some time.

NATURE TELLS YOU.

As Many An Ashville Reader Knows Too Well.

When the kidneys are sick
Nature tells you all about it.
The urine is nature's calendar.
Any urinary trouble tells of kidney ills.
Doan's Kidney Pills cure all kidney ills.
Samuel Stewart, carpenter, of 114 South Liberty street, Spartanburg, S. C., says: "I used Doan's Kidney Pills for my kidney and bladder and for backache, which at the time I thought was rheumatism. I noticed the secretions from the kidneys were strong, very red and looked like jelly on standing for a while and there was much too frequent action, especially at night when I would have to get up out of bed any number of times. The physi..."

Ashville Citizen Times
Tuesday November 7, 1905

Professor Maeda Explains Some Features of the Art of Judo

A graduate of the judo physical culture school of Japan is in the city assisting Professor Ono in his classes. To a representative of the Citizen Times, Professor Maeda explained several matters in connection with Jiu-jitsu and Judo that are not well understood in this country and incidentally threw some light on the class of people engaged in teaching the art in this country. He quoted from an article by a Japanese admirer of the Judo art and said.

"All Japanese are not necessarily Jiu-jitsu experts, just as all Americans are not necessarily wrestlers or prize fighters, or else gentlemen even. Those Japanese who profess Jiu-jitsu in this country are not necessarily entitled to teach it or even say that they know much about it. Just as 30 or 40 years ago, when Japan was eager to secure the services of any English-speaking person to teach the language, some common sailors or even tramps from England or America were teaching English in Japanese schools. Since some foreign newspaper correspondents in Japan began to report wonderful things of this art of self-defense (commonly so-called outside our own country), saying that in Japan there was no man who did not study it, from the Emperor down to the poorest laborers; that this universal practice of Jiu-jitsu was the greatest cause of Japan's victory over Russia as well as of her soldiers' health and sturdiness and so on ad infinitum."

"You Americans have aroused a great deal of curiosity to see the actual thing done before your eyes, hence the results that some young Japanese, who were housework boys or schoolboys until the previous day, whose mere names even were not known amongst his countrymen much less as Jiu-jitsu men, appear on the stage one lucky morning as great masters of the art of pliancy!"

Jiu-jitsu was a genuine product of feudalism in Japan and with the feudalism it practically died 38 years ago when our great revolution took place. Some 15 years later it revived under the name of Judo, after a careful investigation and comparison of all the forms or schools of Ju-jitsu on the part of professor Kano, who has completely remodeled and enlarged the teachings on the physiological and educational basis and through whose zeal and influence this Judo is now introduced into nearly all government schools over and above the Occidental systems of physical training. The old Ju-jitsu aimed at either killing or otherwise controlling one's foe by a mere throw without using any weapon or arresting a criminal without inflicting a wound upon him, or else keeping one's antagonist in such a position as rendered resistance impossible."

"As such a mode of fighting or of self-defense without weapons, it had to resort to the choking of the throat, the twisting of the joints the kicking or hitting of the vital parts, as well as to more forcible throws down on the ground. But the new school of Judo is no longer an art of fighting or of self-defense, but a system of moral culture combined with a special form of physical training. And as such, throat choking, joint twisting, hitting or kicking assumes no prominent feature in it at all. In fact, these dangerous practices are strictly discouraged, though we teach how to escape from these modes of attack. In this glorious century of revolver, machine guns, wireless telegraphy and smokeless gunpowder to teach Ju-jitsu as an art of warfare is of course absurd."

"Matches of Ju-jitsu men versus wrestlers are no less absurd. Ju-jitsu and Judo both aimed at controlling the antagonist with the least expenditure possible of mere brute strength, while in wrestling, either of America or Japan, the main feature is strength more than skill or agility. Because wrestling uses much physical force, wrestlers cannot continue a match very long before they get exhausted, consequently they have to decide the case with a momentary touch of both shoulders to the floor (and in Japanese wrestling a ring of about 15 feet in diameter is used -- to be pushed out of the circle even by half of a foot means defeat, as well as a mere touch on the ground of one finger or elbow or knee.)"

"On the contrary in Ju-jitsu matches, we have to keep the opponent on the mat for a minute or two in an immovable condition: or else we throw our antagonist forcibly on the ground and, in doing so, we may lie down as a means to the end. Then, again as an accomplishment for Samurai or soldier gentlemen of the feudal times, Ju-jitsu presupposes that both parties are properly dressed as respectable people should be, whereas wrestling of America and also of Japan is done in a condition of nudity. From the very nature of the two things, Ju-jitsu men and wrestlers cannot try their skills or strength on a footing of equality it is something like comparing skill and running and riding."

"If, however, both parties can agree on some fair terms by mutual compromise, matches between these two different things may not be altogether uninteresting. But you must expect the result always will be that wrestlers may beat Ju-jitsu men in wrestling ways, but not in Ju-jitsu ways, whereas the latter may succeed in controlling or resisting wrestlers, according to their own standards and which wrestlers themselves may not recognize as their defeat from their own standpoint. Such being the case, American wrestlers cannot much boast of their art if they beat a Ju-jitsu man: for them to try a match with a nameless, mushroom Jiu-jitsuist is nonsense, to say the least of it. If you must have such a performance to satisfy your curiosity, it may not be a bad idea for you to have a preliminary contest between old style Ju-jitsu men and scientific Judo-ists, to see whether such a man as Higashi or Yabe is really entitled or not to call themselves champions and exponents of this unique sort of gentlemanly sport of Japan. You must remember that there are at least half a dozen of true Judo-ists on the Atlantic side of this continent, who have received certificates for their attainments direct from Professor Kano, founder of the modern improved school of judo, by studying for years in his great gymnasium in Tokyo known as the Kodokan which is visited by foreign tourists as one of the rare institutions of our country."

Professor Maeda himself was a student under professor at Kano and believes that as a mode of physical training judo is superior to American methods of physical culture. Asked what he thought of the American style of wrestling, Prof. Maeda said he thought highly of it and admired the skills shown by American wrestlers and matches. He has himself taken part in several exhibitions in American style, but said he did not intend to engage in a match in this city.

Professor Maeda leaves in a few days for New York, where he will take part in an exhibition the latter part of November. He will return here in December and may remain for some time.

Asheville Citizen Times
Wednesday December 13th 1905

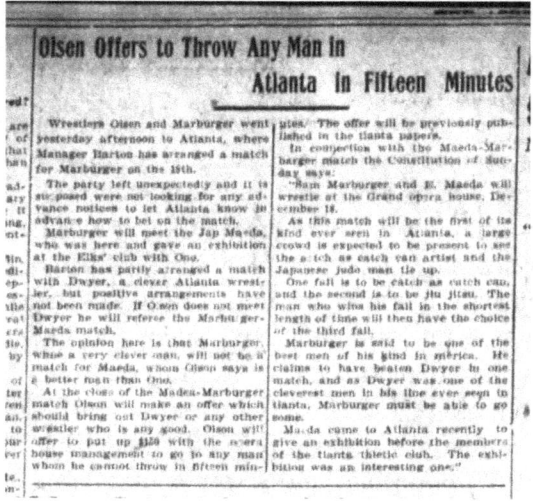

Star Tribune
Sunday February 28th 1909

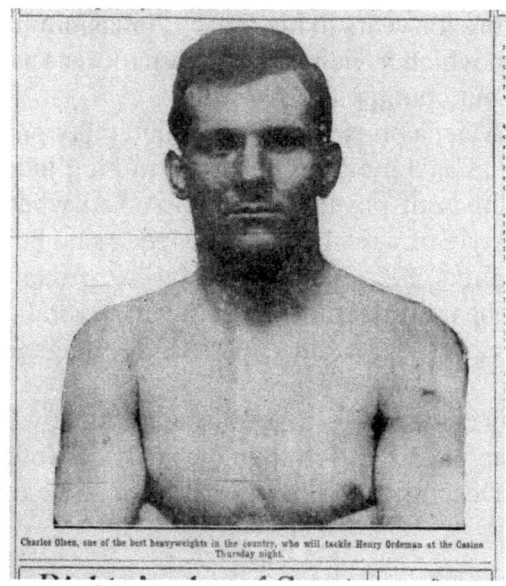

Charles Olsen, one of the best heavyweights in the country, who will tackle Henry Ordeman at the Casino Thursday night

Asheville Citizen Times
Wednesday December 13th 1905

Wrestlers Olson and Marburger went yesterday afternoon to Atlanta, where Manager Burton has arranged a match for Marburger on the 18th. The party left unexpectedly, and it is supposed were not looking for any advance notices to let Atlanta know in advance how to bet on the match.

Marburger will meet the Jap Maeda, who was here and gave an exhibition at the Elks club with Ono.

Burton has partly arranged a match with Dwyer, a clever Atlanta wrestler, but positive arrangements have not been made. If Olson does not meet Dwyer, he will referee the Marburger-Maeda match. The opinion here is that Marburger, while a very clever man, will not be a match for Maeda, whom Olsen says is a better man than Ono.

At the close of the Maeda-Marburger match Olsen will make an offer which should bring out Dwyer or any other wrestler who is any good. Olsen will offer to put up $150 with the Opera House management to go to any man whom he cannot throw in 15 minutes. The offer will be previously published in the Atlanta papers.

In connection with the Maeda-Marburger match the Constitution of Sunday says:

"Sam Marburger and E. Maeda will wrestle at the Grand Opera House, December 18th.

"As this match will be the first of its kind ever seen in Atlanta, a large crowd is expected to be present to see the catch as catch can artist and the Japanese judo man tie up.

One fall is to be catch-as-catch-can, and the second is to be Jujitsu. The man who wins this fall in the shortest length of time will then have the choice of the third fall.

Marburger is said to be one of the best men of his kind in America. He claims to have beaten Dwyer in one match, and as Dwyer was one of the cleverest in his line ever seen in Atlanta, Marburger must be able to go.

Maeda came to Atlanta recently to give an exhibition before the members of the Atlanta Athletic Club the exhibition was an interesting one."

Asheville Citizen Times
Monday Dec 17, 1905

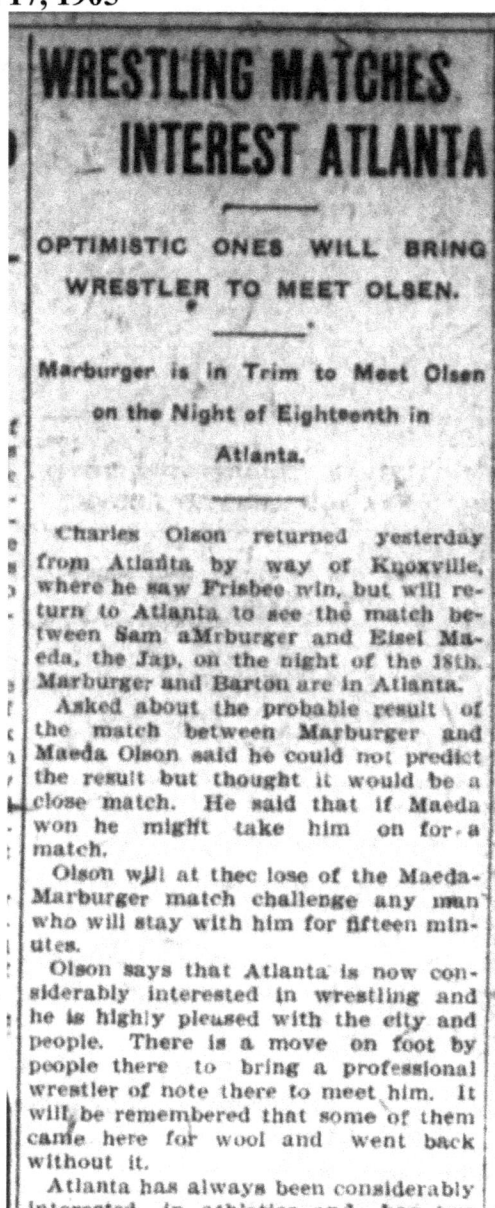

WRESTLING MATCHES INTEREST ATLANTA

OPTIMISTIC ONES WILL BRING WRESTLER TO MEET OLSEN.

Marburger is in Trim to Meet Olsen on the Night of Eighteenth in Atlanta.

Charles Olson returned yesterday from Atlanta by way of Knoxville, where he saw Frisbee win, but will return to Atlanta to see the match between Sam aMrburger and Eisei Maeda, the Jap, on the night of the 18th. Marburger and Barton are in Atlanta.

Asked about the probable result of the match between Marburger and Maeda Olson said he could not predict the result but thought it would be a close match. He said that if Maeda won he might take him on for a match.

Olson will at thec lose of the Maeda-Marburger match challenge any man who will stay with him for fifteen minutes.

Olson says that Atlanta is now considerably interested in wrestling and he is highly pleased with the city and people. There is a move on foot by people there to bring a professional wrestler of note there to meet him. It will be remembered that some of them came here for wool and went back without it.

Atlanta has always been considerably interested in athletics and has two athletic clubs with fine club houses.

Olson and Marburger will be at Hendersonville on the 20th when Marburger meets McKenzie, the sailor.

**Asheville Citizen Times
Monday Dec 17, 1905**

WRESTLING MATCHES INTEREST ATLANTA

Optimistic ones will bring wrestler to meet Olsen

**Marburger is in trim to meet Olsen
on the night of 18th in
Atlanta**

Charles Olsen returned yesterday from Atlanta by way of Knoxville where he saw frisbee win but will return to Atlanta to see the match between Sam Marburger and Eisei Maeda, the Jap, on the night of the 18th. Marburger and Burton are in Atlanta

Asked about the probable results of the match between Marburger and Maida Olsen said he could not predict the results, but he thought it would be a close match. He said that if Maeda won, he might take him on for a match.

Olsen will at the close of the Maeda-Marburger match challenge any man who will stay with him for 15 minutes.

Olsen says that Atlanta is now considerably interested in wrestling, and he is highly pleased with the city and people. There is a move on foot by people there to bring a professional wrestler of note there to meet him. It will be remembered that some of them came here for wool and went back without it. Atlanta has always been considerably interested in athletics and has two athletic clubs with fine club houses.

Olsen and Marburger will be at Hendersonville on the 20th when Marburger meets Mc Kenzie the sailor

**Asheville Citizen Times
December 19th 1905**

MARBURGER LOSE TO JAP WRESTLER

E. Maeda, Formerly of This City Gets Two Falls Out of Three in Bout at Atlanta.

ATLANTA, Ga., Dec. 18.—A wrestling match between S. Marburger, an American, and E. Maeda, an exponent of jiu-jitsu, was held here tonight before an audience that packed the Grand Opera House. The Japanese won the first and third falls in twelve and eighteen minutes respectively. Marburger took the second fall, catch-as-catch-can in twenty-eight minutes.

**Asheville Citizen Times
December 19th 1905**

Marburger lose to Jap Wrestler

E. Maeda, formerly of this city gets two falls out of three in about at Atlanta

　　A wrestling match between S Marburger and American and Maida and exponent of Ju-jitsu was held here tonight before an audience that packed the grand upper house. The Japanese won the first and third falls in 12 and 18 minutes respectively. Marburger took the second full, catch-as-catch-can in 28 minutes

MAEDA MITSUYO・前田光世

The Atlanta Constitution
Tuesday December 19th 1905

SAM MARBURGER LOST TO MAIDA

Little Jap Had All the Best of Wrestling Match at the Grand.

Sam Marburger, the American wrestler, who claims that Mike Dwyer would be easy for him, fell victim last night at the Grand to the jiu-jitsu cunning of Maida, the little Jap.

Outweighed by twenty pounds, at least, the athlete from the Orient carried off all the honors of the evening, and before the finish of the three falls had won the sympathy of the major part of the audience. The first fall was jiu-jitsu, and was won by the Jap in twelve minutes; the second was catch-as-catch-can, and went to the American in twenty-eight minutes, while the third and deciding fall was won by the Jap in eight minutes.

That the match last night was spectacular and pleasing to the eye can not be denied, but those wrestling fans in the crowd last night noted two things that looked a little out of place, to say the least. In the first place, Marburger showed up as the veriest novice at the jiu-jitsu style, while the Jap apparently realized his inability to accomplish anything in the catch-as-catch-can game, and for twenty-five minutes of the twenty-eight was on the defensive.

After the match, Marburger stated that last night was the first time that he had ever tried a jiu-jitsu fall. To the crowd it looked as if he was lifeless, wary and apparently expecting to be thrown every minute.

In the catch-as-catch-can fall, which style of wrestling Atlantans understand better than the jiu-jitsu, Marburger seemed confident of winning, but apparently relied more upon bodily strength and weight than he did upon skill at the game. Once he almost locked a full nelson and then lost it, several times his half nelsons failed to work, while the hammer lock was totally ineffective. The fall which he finally obtained came more as the result of the gradual pressing of his body against that of the lighter Jap than as the result of any particular grip or hold.

Marburger's manager claims that he would have an easy time with Mike Dwyer, who held his own against all comers in Atlanta last year, until beaten by Gotch. If such a match could be arranged, it would undoubtedly prove a drawing card, as Dwyer has many friends in Atlanta who would be willing to back him against Marburger.

The Atlanta Constitution
Tuesday December 19th 1905

Sam Marburger, the American wrestler, who claims that Mike Dwyer would be easy for him, fell victim last night at the grand to the Ju-jitsu cunning of Maeda, the little Japanese

Outweighed by 20 pounds, the athlete from the Orient carried off all the honors of the evening, and before the finish of the three falls had won the sympathy of the major part of the audience. The first fall was Ju-jitsu and was won by the Japanese in 12 minutes. The second was catch-as-catch-can, and went to the American in 28 minutes, while the third and deciding fall was won by the Japanese in eight minutes.

That the match last night was spectacular and pleasing to the eye cannot be denied, but those wrestling fans in the crowd last night noted two things that looked a little out of place, to say the least. In the first place, Marburger showed up as the novice at the Ju-jitsu style, while the Jeff apparently realized his inability to accomplish anything in the catch-as-catch-can game, and for 25 minutes of the 28 was on the defensive.

After the match, Marburger stated that last night was the first time he had ever tried a Ju-jitsu fall period to the crowd it looked as if he was lifeless, weary and apparently expecting to be thrown every minute.

New York Tribune
Thursday February 8th 1906

JUDO FOR SELF-DEFENCE

Methods of Japanese Fighting Entertain a Big Crowd.

There were six hundred spectators in the Columbia University gymnasium last night to see an exhibition of Judo and two-handed sword fighting by six Japanese experts. These men were brought to America by E. H. Harriman, who became interested in this style of fighting on his trip to the Far East.

The most amusing thing on the programme was a two-handed sword fight between Isogaya and Mizutani, a boy eleven years old. When the fighters appeared they were dressed in short skirts and shirts and wore on their heads something that bore a strong resemblance to a women's sunbonnet. They were both masked and liberally padded. After the preliminaries, consisting of an extended salaam, the hostilities began. With bamboo swords they beat each other unmercifully about the head, shoulders and thighs. When they got fairly started they reminded the spectators of two old women belaboring each other over the head with broomsticks. Occasionally they varied the monotony by deftly rolling each other over on their backs and rubbing their swords across each other's throats. All the time there came from the field of battle sounds which the spectators were entirely unable to define. At times it sounded like the quacking of a duck. Some thought that they were inviting each other to come on. Others said it was the Japanese way of swearing.

Before the exercise in judo began Mr. Moriya, Editor of "The Japanese Times," explained the difference between jiu jitsu and judo. He said:

Judo is an improved form of jiu jitsu. In it science is brought into play, and a close knowledge of anatomy is necessary for success in the art. It is much less brutal than boxing, wrestling or your American game of football. In judo, the aim is to kill your opponent or at least to disable him for life. For the complete success of the art a stone pavement or something of the kind is necessary. Judo was invented for the purpose of defence when an unarmed man meets one with a sword or a spear.

After his introduction Messrs. Maeda and Sumi appeared on the mat, barefooted and clad in white kimonos and short, baggy trousers. After a preliminary bow the bout was on. To the spectator it looked as if most of the falls were prearranged before the match. Maeda would walk up to Sumi and grab him by the arm or collar, and Sumi would obediently fall to the mat with a heavy thud. In the second round both tried some defensive work, and showed some clever foot movements. Falls were less frequent, and came after one man had obtained a hold which would either break a bone or send the man flying to the mat.

Mr. Tomita and Maeda then gave an exhibition of the more advanced form of judo defence. Maeda would rush up and make a vicious swing, which invariably stopped just before it reached the other man's head. Tomita would then grab his opponent by the arm or throat and swing him to the mat. Sumi and Maeda also gave an exhibition of sword fighting, which, while it was not so amusing, appeared more scientific than the other bout. Any spectator who doubted the ability of the Japs was invited to try conclusions with one of them, but none of the Columbia wrestlers seemed willing to accept.

WOOD ALCOHOL KILLS SOLDIER.

Prisoners in Castle Williams Drink Wood Alcohol—One Dies, Others Ill.

New York Tribune
Thursday February 8th 1906

Methods of Japanese fighting entertaining a big crowd

There were 600 spectators in the Columbia University gymnasium last night to see an exhibition of judo and two-handed sword fighting by 6 Japanese experts. These men were brought to America by E.H. Harriman who became interested in this style of fighting on his trip to the Far East.

The most amusing thing on the program was a two-handed sword fight between Jsogaya and Mizutani, a boy 11 years old. When the fighters appeared they were dressed in short skirts and shirts and wore on their heads something that bore a strong resemblance to a woman's sunbonnet. They were both masked and liberally padded. After the preliminaries, consisting of an extended Salaam, the hostilities began. With bamboo swords they beat each other unmercifully about the head, shoulders and thighs. When they got fairly started, they reminded the spectators of two old women belaboring each other over the head with broomsticks. Occasionally they varied the monotony by deftly rolling each other over on their backs and rubbing their swords across each other's throats. All the time there came from the field of battle sounds which the spectators were entirely unable to define. At times it sounded like the quacking of a duck. Some thought that they were inviting each other to come on. Others said it was the Japanese way of swearing.

Before the exercise in judo began Mr. Morita, editor of the Japanese Times came on explain the difference between Jiu-jitsu and judo. He said:

"Judo is an improved form of Jiu-jitsu. In it science is brought into play, and a close knowledge of anatomy is necessary for success in the arts it is much less brutal than boxing, wrestling or your American game of football. In Judo, the aim is to kill your opponent or at least disable him for life. For the complete success of the art a stone pavement or something of the kind is necessary. Judo was invented for the purpose of defense when an unarmed man meets one with a sword or a spear."

After his introduction Messrs. Maeda and Sumi appeared on the mat, barefooted and clad in white kimonos and short, baggy trousers. after a preliminary bow the bout was on. To the spectators it looked as if most of the falls were prearranged before the match. Maeda would walk up to Sumi and grab him by the arm or collar, and Sumi would obediently fall to the mat with a heavy thud. In the second round both tried some clever defensive work and showed some clever foot movements. Falls were less frequent and came after one man had obtained a hold which would either break a bone or send the man flying to the mat.

Mr. Tomita and Maeda a then gave an exhibition of the more advanced form of Judo defense. Maeda would rush up and make a vicious swing, which invariably stopped just before it reached the other man's head. Tomita would then grab his opponent by the arm or throat and swing him to the mat. Sumi and Maeda also gave an exhibition of sword fighting, which, while it was not so amusing, appeared more scientific than the other bouts. Any spectators who doubted the ability of the Japs was invited to try conclusions with one of them, but none of the Columbia wrestlers seemed willing to accept.

The Brooklyn Daily Eagle Sun
October 14th 1906

> SPECIAL FRENCH classes begin October 29; two lessons a week, Mondays and Fridays, at 3 P.M.; small classes; by Monsieur RENE SAMSON, of the Teaching Corps, Polytechnic Institute, 85 Livingston st, near Court.
> o14 3t su
>
> **JUJITSU.**
> Instructed by Professors Maeda and Kyono, formerly instructors of military college and Doshisha University, Japan. Address 190 High st, Brooklyn.
>
> **BEDFORD ACADEMY,**
> 640 NOSTRAND AV.
> School for boys and girls, with kindergarten; 21st year. DR. GEORGE RODEMANN, Prin.
>
> NOW OPEN. STERN'S SCHOOL OF
> **LANGUAGES,**
> 177-179 Montague St.
> Class or private lessons.
>
> PRIVATE lessons; English, Latin, mathematics, college, regents' preparation; pupils unsuccessful in school; either home; reasonable; references. WALDRON, VASSAR, 857 Union street.
>
> OSTEOPATHY. Correspondence course, with D. O. College degree, $50 cash, option of practical training; very reasonable. Correspondence Department, Vitus Academia, Philadelphia, Pa.

Jiu-jitsu
Instructed by Professors Maeda and Kyono, formerly instructors of military college and (at?) Doshisha (Waseda?), University, Japan. Address 190 High St, Brooklyn

www.ingramcontent.com/pod-product-compliance
Lightning Source LLC
Chambersburg PA
CBHW050632160426
43194CB00010B/1639